THE HEART

OF

SUCCESS

GROWING YOUR PROFESSIONAL AND
PERSONAL LIFE THE RIGHT WAY!

KEITH D. WASHO

EVOLVE

The Heart of Success: Growing Your Professional and Personal Life the Right Way!
Featuring Interviews with Silicon Valley Executives

978-0-9916229-3-1 Paperback
978-0-9916229-4-8 Ebook

Edited by: Tony Held
Author Photograph by Sean Duan, www.seanduan.com

Published by Evolve Publishing, Inc.
www.evolvepublishing.com

Printed in the United States of America
First edition March 2015

10 9 8 7 6 5 4 3 2 1

Dedication

This book is dedicated to all my colleagues in Silicon Valley, the executives who participated in this book, and my classmates from State University of New York at Oswego, University of Miami, and Saint Mary's College of California. Additionally, to all my friends and family who supported me throughout the years.

Furthermore, this book is dedicated to my father, Michael Washo. Thank you for inspiring me with all your creativity and the spirit of being productive. Thank you for your love and for leaving us with your art, books, gardening and landscaping, success advice, and wonderful family.

Lastly, this book is dedicated to you the reader. I hope it serves as a guiding light and helpful resource to your personal life and professional career.

Contents

Foreword

I got to know Keith as a student in my Executive MBA class. He came to class prepared, having read the assigned material, done the assignments and ready to engage with his peers in lively discussions with his thought through questions and comments. He demonstrated his active mind, along with the ability and discipline to work hard to apply it productively.

The book is a personal labor of love where Keith manifests these same qualities. You are invited to join Keith in his personal quest for articulating what success is, and how to attain and maintain it. You get to listen in on his conversations with Silicon Valley executives he admires as he uncovers the lessons from their experiences, and gets their favorite quotes for ongoing inspiration. He distils it further to get to the bottom line with his wisdom, often presented gently and pithily with his graphic art spread throughout the book.

The title rightfully has the word heart in it. Keith covers not just career advancement, successful products or the implicit definition of success as the accumulation of wealth or glory, but also the often neglected elements of success that are about having faith and a healthy lifestyle with family, friendships, and time to play. Recently, we attended a dialog at my son's high school titled "Challenge Success" where stressed high school children learned about the importance of "PDF," i.e., Personal time, Down time and Family time. This expansion of what success truly means is reason alone to recommend this book.

I happen to believe that thoughtful people ultimately come to their own definition of success. In this account of Keith's sincere and earnest distillation, based on his wide and deep search, you may find your own answers, or material to make you pause and question your own ideas of success or inspiration to start on your journey to synthesize what guides your choices. Along with his opinions and advice, Keith also recommends that the reader go to a marketing textbook to learn the specifics of the 5Ps of marketing or to case studies of technology battles, such as the one between Blu-Ray and HD-DVD, to learn how innovation succeeds, among other sources.

Keith's mission is to pass on his wisdom and values, based on his experiences. In sharing it he honors those from whom he has learned much, be it his father or peers, famous people or pop culture icons. Those lucky enough to be successful say that they got luckier as they persevered with their hard work. Those of you who know Keith already know to read the book based on his hard work. And those of you who don't know him, here is a way to learn though his words, straight from head, heart, and hands.

Jyoti Bachani
Mountain View, CA
5 June 2014

About Dr. Jyoti Bachani

Dr. Bachani is an Associate Professor at Saint Mary's College of California where she teaches courses in strategy and management of technology and innovation. She is a Fulbright Scholar, Editor-in-Chief of an online case-collection and a board member of North American Case Research Association. A published author of many articles, cases, and a book on managing nonprofits, Dr. Bachani studied at the University of Delhi, Stanford University, and the London Business School. She has previously taught at the University of Redlands and San Francisco State. She also has several years of experience as a strategy consultant to Fortune 200 companies, working with Strategic Decisions Group.

Acknowledgement of Contributors

This book aims to show you how to succeed and how to build your success in the right way. To offer you this wisdom I assembled a very specific accomplished group of executives. I selected these specific executives for three main reasons. First off, all the executives interviewed are people I worked with professionally, know personally, or were highly recommended from people I trust. Secondly, they all work in Silicon Valley and have demonstrated successful careers in leading companies, managing people, and achieving results for their organizations. And lastly and most importantly, I sought out executives who also demonstrated that success is not just about your job, career, and finances, but rather a wholesome form of success where family and personal life achievements are just as important as your business endeavors. And this is the type of success that this book is all about. You can understand the linkage when you read the biography section at the end of this book. It gives you more color on who these executives are and our relationship. I'm confident you will gain great practical advice on achieving success in the right way based on the executive insights shared throughout the book and my supporting information.

A special thanks to the executives for their wisdom and advice. This book became possible because these executives took time to participate in interviews and share their knowledge on success. Thanks to these executives, hopefully this book will serve as a guiding light to you and lead you to a more successful career and fulfilling personal life!

Part One:
Introduction

Thesis

Thesis: A statement or theory that is put forward as a premise to be maintained or proved.

This book proposes there is a great kind of success that can be identified and understood. A true success that rises above success's many false imitations. If these great success traits are known, emulated, and then put into action it can help one enjoy a successful life both professionally and personally.

This book aims to share with you this great kind of success based on wisdom shared from executives in Silicon Valley who have proven success in their own lives and insights the author has collected to help further support the advice provided.

The word *success* can mean many things to different people. To write a book on success it's important to define what it is. What is success? This book is based on a specific type of success: the great kind. Good is the enemy of great so it's important to know the difference. What is the great kind of success this book aims to share with you? The type of success this book describes and hopes to impart is well-balanced, tried and true, and built from the ground up on top of a solid foundation that is based on right principles, values, behaviors, and decisions. This type of success comprises of personal and professional achievements that lead to the betterment of yourself, your relationships, your family and friends, the company you work for, and the world around you. You could call it the "Wholesome" or "Whole Hearted" type of success that does it all in the right way. It is success that shines a light and leaves a good example of what being a good person and great contributor to society is. Business leaders such as Henry Ford, George Eastman, Mary Kay, and J.W. Marriott exemplify this type of success. These individuals led successful careers that left a good legacy of value for their families, friends, and the businesses they started, managed, and grew to respectable firms.

This book focuses on this type of success specifically from Silicon Valley executives who have achieved healthy, sustainable careers leading companies amidst the worlds' most dynamic and fast paced business environments. You could say these Silicon Valley executives are like the Henry Ford and George Eastman of today. In the Valley you don't become successful unless you're on top of your game, constantly innovating, reflecting, improving, and delivering results. Operating within the competitive business climate of Silicon Valley can lead to a unique perspective on success. This book shares this perspective with you through wisdom and insights gained from executives who worked the long and hard hours to lead the way. They all "carried the bag."

This book is not about the second-rate form of success that is fleeting or appearing good from the outside, but hollow inside and unsustainable. For example, it's not about an overnight success philosophy. Eddie Cantor spoofed this overnight success myth when he said, "It takes 20 years to make an overnight success!" Additionally, this book is not about the second-rate form of success known as the "get rich, get it all quick" approach either. This type of scheme can leave you high and dry. And lastly, this book is not about a second-rate form of success that is gained through actions or a methodology that brings favor to one at the expense of another or to fortune that is achieved to the detriment of your own health. Richard Baker negates this approach with this wise quote: "To get rich never risk your health. For it is the truth that health is the wealth of wealth."

To substantiate what this poor type of success is with a clear explanation, think of the movie that came out in

2012 called *The Wolf of Wall Street*. This film was based on the true story of Jordan Belfort, a stockbroker and firm owner who rose to fame and "Success" in the 1990s. In short, Jordan was making millions on Wall Street. He had tons of money, power, glamour, glitz, wealth, women, friends, parties, and business. However, this form of success quickly collapsed and evaporated. Why? Because it was hollow, fake, unsustainable, and built upon a foundation of dark shifting sand. Jordan and his firm ended up losing it all to securities fraud and corruption. What appeared to be a success was simply a counterfeit. It was built upon unethical behavior rooted in greed that led to illegal actions that hurt many people along the way. Make no bones about it. This is the bad type of success and there is a clear distinction.

One definition of success this book's message aims to hit is Ralph Waldo Emerson's perspective: "To laugh often and much; to win the respect of intelligent people and the affection of children; to earn the appreciation of honest critics and endure the betrayal of false friends. To appreciate beauty; to find the best in others; to leave the world a bit better whether by a healthy child, or a garden patch or a redeemed social condition; to know that even one life has breathed easier because you have lived. This is to have succeeded."

To achieve the type of success noted by Emerson it's important to know the ingredients that make up this great kind and separate it from the falsities of the bad kind. Understanding this true form of success and the pillars that construct it will guide you to being the right type of person.

Understanding the great kind of success opens up the door to the next phase of putting it all together. This next step is called "knowing thyself." Having good discernment on where you are as person, what you aspire to be, and the gaps in-between provides the ingredients you need to charter your path. Knowing what you are here for will ultimately set you on the right course for your life. It's also healthy to have a good understanding of things you can and cannot control. This will keep you well-balanced and living with the right perspective as you grow in your success. A good quote relevant to knowing thyself and a healthy perspective on what you can and can't control is the serenity prayer by the American theologian Renhold Niebur:

"God, grant me the serenity to accept the things I cannot change, the courage to change the things I can, and the wisdom to know the difference."

To know thyself, you must ask yourself some hard questions and do an honest assessment. For example, are you using the gifts and talents you have been blessed with? Are you achieving your potential? Are you living fully alive? These are the type of questions that will align you correctly for your personal best and help guide you to being at the right place at the right time for your ultimate destiny. The last thing you want to do is climb the ladder of success to realize it's leaning against the wrong wall. This book aims to help you climb the right ladder and have it leaning against the right wall.

The core thesis of this book is to help you gain a healthy understanding of the great form of success and the right ways to achieve it. The book gives you this through insights from Silicon Valley executives who embody this great kind of success. They are executives who lead some of the most innovative tech companies in the world yet have done so with class. I'm excited to provide you their wisdom, learning lessons, and advice—all of which can help you become this great kind of success. These lessons, while geared to helping you better understand success from a Silicon Valley executive's perspective, can also be applied to your life no matter where you live and work. In the song "New York, New York," Frank Sinatra sings about succeeding in New York City. He says, "If you can make it there, you can make it anywhere." If you can understand the principles of achieving success in Silicon Valley, you can apply it to succeeding anywhere indeed.

Please don't accept the advice shared in this book at face value just because a successful person said it; rather read through the lines to explore how the wisdom touches your heart and is valuable to you. Think about how you can apply it to improve your career and life. I encourage you to take time reading through this book. Pause, reflect, and think through the golden nuggets shared. It's packed with insights to be valuable to you quickly, but the knowledge is meant to be savored slowly.

Overall, I hope this book serves as an insightful and fun read to help you get to the top! Furthermore, I hope this book helps you get to your pinnacle in the right way with the right results. Enjoy!

"Ability may get you to the top, but it takes character to keep you there."

—John Wooden, Basketball Coach

Part Two:
Two Ears and One Mouth

This section of the book is about listening and how it plays a paramount role in your success. The three areas explored in this section are the importance of listening, how to be a good listener, and helping others listen to you.

If you ever wondered if it's best to talk or listen more, this quote from Diogenes Laertius, famous biographer of Greek philosophers, says it all, "We have two ears and only one tongue in order that we may hear more and speak less." I hope this section helps bring home for you the importance of listening more than we speak. It's in doing so that we become primed for success!

Chapter 1.
Why Listening is Important

"The most basic and powerful way to connect to another person is to listen. Just listen. Perhaps the most important thing we ever give each other is our attention... A loving silence often has far more power to heal and to connect than the most well-intentioned words."

—Rachel Naomi Remen

There is a reason why the subject of listening is the first chapter. Listening is specifically important in Silicon Valley where thousands of ideas on tech innovation, new products, and new companies are discussed every day. The big venture capital (VC) firms get a new pitch every day. They have to listen intently to identify the next big thing within thirty minutes and can usually get to the point within three minutes. In return, entrepreneurs and tech innovators always listen to what's hot, new, and trending that impacts their business along with adapting to VC and other partner feedback. So listening in some ways is everything in the Valley. If ideas are currency then communicating them and listening is the means of transacting. If you gain the right influence and "buy in" it leads to the big payday, so listening intently is the key to unlocking your full potential.

When I interviewed the executives, listening was ranked as a top contributor to a successful career and personal life. Bottom line: Good listening is very important to your success. For example, when I met with Harry Dickinson, CEO of Fission Stream Technologies, one of his top advice points was the importance of listening. Harry noted, "Good listening skills is directly tied to good management and being successful with people. You need to be a people person and must have good listening skills to succeed." Harry elaborated, "To be successful, you have to listen. It all starts there. Listen to customers. Listen to the market. And listen to the street!" Harry climbed the ladder of success leading many sales teams at global tech companies. It's this skill of good listening that he admits helped him get to the top. Think about it, there is no other means to better understand what is going on with your customers and the world around you than by listening. Only in being aware and listening on all fronts can you absorb the most useful information that can benefit your view of reality and help you identify the right actions needed to address the challenges and opportunities before you.

Another executive who said listening was a top contributor to his overall success was Mark Adams, President of Micron Technologies. Mark said, "You have to be a good listener. It's part of being good with people and showing respect. To be successful you need to be competent and a problem solver. Good listening can help you do that." When Mark was leading sales at Creative Labs he used to have meetings with all his sales team members. He would ask very insightful and direct questions in these sessions. You could tell he was always digging for the bottom line and truth of the situation. He did not settle for "fluff" answers. Through his great listening and probing questions he gained the insights needed to manage the sales team effectively and take proper actions to grow the business, which led to great results for the company.

Another reason why listening is important was offered by Russell Brady, Director of Corporate Communications at Adobe. Russell stated simply, "Listen because listening leads to better decisions." Think about it logically. The more inputs you gain through deep listening, the better understanding you have of any given situation. The more accurate assessment you have of the opportunity or challenge before you, the more clearly you can make correct informed decisions that lead to a higher likelihood of success. Russell has been successful in corporate communications in part because he listens intently to all the inputs around him and then forms a more on-target strategy based upon this knowledge.

Joe Weber, Senor Director of Product Line Management at NeoPhotonics Corporation, offered this reason why listening is so important to your success. Joe stated, "Recognize that people are more likely to implement their own ideas than other people's ideas. By listening to their interests, needs, and ideas you can better have your ideas be their ideas. This helps you move forward on your aims too. Listen to them, include them, and get them engaged." I believe this is a great epiphany on why listening is so important. In short, listening can help you get what you want by aligning it with other people's aims. You will be amazed how often people desire the same things as you and are on the same page with your business objectives. A win-win path can always be found. The key is to listen first before sharing your ideas. Stephen Covey hits this point home:

"Seek first to understand, then to be understood."

I worked with Harry Dickinson at the start-up Bigfoot Networks when he was Executive VP of Sales. He provided a good example on listening. At Bigfoot Networks I recall vividly his patience in trying to understand the retail sales dynamics and asking insightful questions about the channel business. You could tell he really cared and was listening intently by the way he looked at you as if soaking in your every word. He was like a sponge. This good type of listening leads you to success because it brings forth more clearly all the relevant information. It also makes both people feel comfortable sharing openly and honestly. This type of intent listening is referred to by psychologists as attentive or active listening.

Attentive and active listening create a powerful winning combo for all parties involved. First, the person communicating benefits from the intent listening because it makes the person feel valued, respected, and comfortable. It makes one open up to share more freely. This makes the message flow out more deeply and effectively for the listener to gain more of the meaning. Secondly, the listener benefits tremendously because more information is shared and can be absorbed more clearly for better retention. Lastly, it builds up a great rapport between both persons communicating.

All sales people know that listening to your customer sincerely and intently is the leading contributor to sales success. Good listening enables you to better understand your client's needs, show your customers you care, gain important insights needed to create great products that best serve the customer, and ultimately build great relationships that increase your sales. Toby Preston, Senior Director of Sales at Qualcomm, lives and dies by sales. Some of his most important success advice was around listening. He noted, "Listen up! In order to get people to listen to you, you must first be willing to show respect and listen to them. Listen to people and absorb information. You learn most from others." I have been in numerous sales meeting with Toby and every time he listens more than he speaks and opens up the floor for dialog. He listens. He asks good questions and takes notes. It's no surprise he has been able to rise to Senior Director of Sales for one of the biggest tech companies in the world. His listening skills are great and make every meeting more productive.

Lastly, listening is important because we learn and gain valuable information. Plus it makes you more likeable. As Wilson Mizner notes,

"A good listener is not only popular everywhere, but after a while he gets to know something."

Listening is also important because it shows people you care and respect them. Listening injects goodness into all your relationships. Being a good listener is an essential ingredient to all and makes up the heart of success.

"It is the province of knowledge to speak and it is the privilege of wisdom to listen"

—Oliver Wendell Holmes

 Executive Corner

- Do you seek first to understand, then to be understood?

- In order to get people to listen to you, you must first be willing to show respect and listen to them.

- Listen, because listening leads to better decisions.

Chapter 2.
Being an Effective Listener

"The most basic of all human needs is the need to under-
stand and be understood. The best way to understand
people is to listen to them."

—Ralph Nichols

We established in Chapter 1 that listening is an important pillar to your success. There is a litany of benefits to being a good listener as the previous chapter alluded to. In short, all the data supports the thesis that listening helps you learn more, capture information more accurately, and demonstrate to the person your conversing with that you really care. Good listening primes you for success.

You're probably wondering, "What are the keys to being a good listener then?" I asked the executives this exact question in all the interviews. Here is a summary of their responses so you can learn from their advice on listening effectively.

Most of the executives commented that to be a good listener it's important to hear not only what is being said, but to read body language and to hear tone of the voice too. This can tell you more about what someone really feels and thinks. Charles Whyte, Senior Director at Western Digital, elaborated on this point when he suggested "... listen **not only to what** is being said, but **how** it's being said." Whyte's quote stresses the importance of reading the vocal tone and body language of the people you're conversing with. For example, if the pitch of the person's voice goes higher or moves at a faster rate it can be a sign that the speaker is uncomfortable with the subject at hand or is skirting around the truth. In addition, nonverbal communication experts have documented that if someone's arms are crossed when talking it's a sign she may be uncomfortable or holding information back. Also, if someone shuns eye contact and looks away in the conversation at specific points it can be a sign that he's distorting the truth. By hearing and reading these communication signs you are empowered to better read the reality of the situation.

Furthermore, it allows you to adjust your communication style and conversation to focus on areas that may need further addressing to build more trust. Also, by listening to the way things are being said it can help you identify areas that may need more vetting out to hit the true heart of the matter. Charles is not only a successful tech executive, he's also a professional musician.

This tip on listening to not only what is being said, but how it's being said applies well to the music world. In music you don't just listen to the lyrics. You listen to both the music and lyrics together and that evokes a specific emotion. Listening to both is what helps you capture the true meaning of the song. This is similar to how it works when listening to people. To get the most accurate understanding of the communication you need to listen to both the verbal and visual message being sent.

The famous management guru, Peter F. Drucker, stated another important perspective about listening:

"The most important thing in communication is to hear what isn't being said."

You can call this reading between the lines and connecting the dots. *Popular Science* states that 93 percent of all daily communication is nonverbal. Dr. Albert Mehrabian, author of *Silent Messages*, conducted several studies on nonverbal communication. He found that seven percent of any message is conveyed through words, 38 percent through certain vocal elements, and 55 percent through nonverbal elements (facial expressions, gestures, posture, etc). If you take away the seven percent for the words that actually leave someone's mouth, 93 percent of all communication is nonverbal With the majority of the message meaning being conveyed nonverbally, it's critical you listen with your eyes wide open. One metaphor to help you conceptualize how to listen most effectively is to think of listening with your eyes. If you're typing while listening or reading something while someone is trying to communicate with you, you're missing some of the most important parts of the communication. Look carefully for nonverbal signals. Listen with your eyes!

The other key to being a good listener is the

importance of staying quiet. As Harry Dickinson noted, "Be the last to speak. Listen to everyone. Then coalesce what everyone said and then give your input." It's amazing how smart you can appear when you repeat back in a succinct fashion some of the wisdom already shared in the conversation and then add your own unique insights to it. You can also provide value to the conversation by connecting the dots of the most important parts communicated and pointing out the key elements that can be actionable. For example, "Based on what we discussed we know the importance of A, B, and C so we need to make sure we do E, F, and G." On the flip side, Charles Whyte noted, "Sometimes it's good to just be quiet. Listen. If you don't know something then keep quiet." Abraham Lincoln brings this point to life by explaining the goodness that comes from being silent at times,

"It's better to be quiet and be assumed a fool, than to speak and remove all doubt."

Matt Kaufman, President of CrunchBase, said something interesting about how to listen effectively. Matt noted, "You can learn a lot by listening to others when you ask two key questions. What can I do to better help you? What can our organization and team do to better help the company?" Matt said these two questions can help open up very valuable conversations and ensure you better understand the most important needs of your people and organization. Lastly, Matt suggested that to get ahead through listening, "Be open to criticism and seek out information to improve." It's by asking and listening to this constructive feedback that you get a reality check on how you are really performing and what is needed. Armed with this information you can deliver better results that address what is really lacking. Additionally, Matt suggested some advice on how to listen effectively by suggesting face-to-face interactions versus phone calls. "Sitting across from someone affords great dialog, respect, trust, and openness plus creates a great learning environment when you can get people together in the same room. In addition, always go into a conversation as peers with mutual respect. Go in with an open mind that you truly have just as much to learn from the other person as they do from you too."

Listening effectively is an art form and takes practice. As Kevin Conley, SVP and GM at SanDisk, noted, "Invest time to be good at listening. Take coaching." Kevin provided this additional insight on effective listening, "Practice active listening by repeating back what is being said. Restating it helps you understand and shows the person that they are being heard and understood." Lastly, Kevin suggested this point: "Listen to others knowing you can't be right all the time. And be prepared to identify good information from unlikely sources. This is known as wisdom from the mouth of babes."

I love this "mouth of babes" reference as it's very insightful. It even has biblical roots. "Out of the mouths of babes", is essentially a metaphor that refers to the idea that even the young and the naive can spout wisdom. For example, if a young child were listening to two adults shouting at each other and said, "They would get along a lot better if they stopped shouting and starting listening more," someone might respond to that by saying, "Out of the mouths of babes." This implies that the child showed more wisdom than the adults. The point is to listen to all people respectfully and equally. You may find a golden nugget of wisdom and truth sprouting from the most unassuming sources.

Craig McHugh, CEO of Cambridge SoundWorks, also noted that listening is a skill you have to hone and build. You really need to try hard and focus on it. He suggested one key action to helping you listen more effectively is to take notes. Craig stated, "Take good notes to help you remember. Ask questions and note the most important points and key take-aways. Stop and give good attention when listening. Show you care and respect what is being said." Almost all the executives stressed the importance of taking notes during conversations as one of the best ways to really listen. Especially in sales, where note taking is key to capturing all the customer feedback plus showing you really care about what they have to say. This is a "must do" tip for your listening success!

One of the most unique tips on effective listening

came from Richard Sanquini, Chairman of PixelWorks. He suggested envisioning listening as a step process and in stages. Richard recommended, "First listen to fully understand. Summarize what you hear and ask basic clarifying questions. Listen carefully to everything said to form a solid basis. Then ask challenging questions to gain deeper insights as the next step of the listening process."

If you think of listening in this perspective, you can imagine peeling a proverbial onion, where you move from the outer layer of generalities and top line understanding to a deeper layer with more specifics. Peeling the onion brings you from a top level understanding to a deeper grasp of the most important fundamentals. The key is to not shoot straight for the core or jump to conclusions via assumptions. Make sure you build a sound basis from going through the first step of peeling the outer layers to gain an accurate top level understanding. Lastly, Richard gave these points on effective listening, "Listen to as many people as possible. Free yourself to make quality time to listen. Be engaged and alert. Start with the notion that you have no idea so your mind is fully open. Finally, when you listen make sure you stop to digest, summarize, and ask questions. You must concentrate and internalize all."

A unique perspective on listening was offered up by Sam Nicolino, President and CEO of Adaptive Sound Technologies. Sam noted, "Yes listening is important, but be careful of listening too much. You can't please everyone and take all the advice. You need to also have good selective hearing. Listen, process, discern, and then don't jump to conclusions. If something doesn't resonate after listening and fully thinking about it, drop it and move on." This insight is very helpful because when it comes to gaining advice from people and listening accordingly, you will encounter various forms of suggestions that will vary in direction. The key is to absorb it, think about it, but then ultimately do what you believe is the right action. You can't try to please everyone by doing what they suggest. The famous comedian Bill Cosby said it best,

> *"I don't know the key to success, but the key to failure is trying to please everybody."*

All the executives shared the importance of face-to-face interactions and making time for in-person meetings as the most effective way to open up conversations and have the best environment for effective listening. Phone calls and emails can only do so much. If possible, take the time to meet with people in person to discuss important business matters. The executives emphasized the importance of one-on-one meetings as paramount to your listening success. So get off your phone and your email. Go meet with people and talk in person. It does listening good!

"Listening for and identifying the tone in others and adapting appropriately — as well being conscious of the tone of your own messages — will determine your communication effectiveness. Being tone conscious will prevent you from sending and receiving messages that fall on deaf ears. Sometimes the most revealing part of a message isn't found in the words themselves but in the subtle messages wrapped around those words. Failure to pick up on these 'secret messages' may leave you blind to what is really being communicated."

—Dianne Boohe

Executive Corner

- Do you practice active listening?

- Listen not only to what is being said, but how it's being said.

- Sometimes it's good to be the last to speak. Absorb all and then chime in!

Chapter 3.
Helping Others Listen To You

"Earn the right to be heard by listening to others. Seek to understand a situation before making judgments about it."

—John Maxwell

In the previous chapters we reviewed the importance of listening effectively in order to be successful. The next important aspect in your career advancement and leadership persona is the ability to get others to listen to you. In Silicon Valley, ideas are currency. The ability to get someone to really listen to you and buy into your ideas can be the difference between winning and losing. When people buy into your currency of ideas it is equivalent to a payday.

Why is getting others to listen to you so important? Because when people listen to you, you have the best opportunity to influence, lead, and affect change. Where is this concept proven true? Look at the leaders you like most, trust, and are willing to follow. Are they the type of people who make it easy for you to listen and be open to their ideas? Point proven!

In order to help people listen to you it's important to understand human dynamics. I have found the essence of getting others to listen is simply this: Be the type of person who others want to listen to. You may have heard the words *command respect*. People listen to those they respect. How do you get people to respect you? The key is to be a person of real substance and good character who gives real value. Then people will genuinely like you, respect you, and be open to listening to you. Joe Castillo, GM at Acer Computers, suggested this: "Bring value and deliver something that helps others and they will want to listen. Understand their needs and be able to communicate something that addresses their wants. Bring new and insightful information and people will listen." For example, if you have a meeting coming up, bring to the table some new data points or intelligence that helps add extra value to the discussion.

Harry Dickinson, CEO of Fission Stream Technologies, noted that to help others listen to you it's important to do one big thing: Always make it about them. Ask the people you are conversing with the following types of questions: What do you want? What do you need? How can I help you succeed and reach your goals? With these types of questions asked to understand and serve people, you can gather the key information you need to develop your message around their interests. They will then want to listen to you because it's all about them!

Matt Kaufman, President of CrunchBase, suggested that to get others to listen to you, it's key to respect them and show you care. Be a peer. Based on all the executive input I received, the evidence shows this to be true. Respect others and show sincere interest in them. In return, it helps others be more open to listening to you. Toby Preston, Senior Director of Sales at Qualcomm, backed up this point by sharing this sentiment: "Show respect and listen to others. In order to get people to listen to you, you must first be willing to show respect and listen to them. Take notes. It helps you remember and shows respect for others too." This reminds me of a quote by John Maxwell,

> *"People don't care how much you know until they know how much you care."*

Dick Sanquini, Chairman of PixelWorks, really hit this point home too. Dick said, "In order to get others to listen to you, you must listen to them first. Engage others and get their inputs. Welcome them in with questions, listen, and show respect and show you care. Then you can get them to listen to you after they know you listened to them and have their inputs taken into consideration and their best interests at heart too." This is why sales training experts often suggest you start off your meetings by expressing interest in the people you're meeting with. Open up with some questions to get them to talk first. Then transition into information you have prepared to help serve them.

Sam Nicolino, President and CEO of Adaptive Sound Technologies, had an easy suggestion on getting others to listen to you: "Yelling!" All jokes aside, Sam shared his thoughts on creating an environment for good listening. Sam said, "Going to the black board and showing a visual of your idea or concept helps others listen to you and understand. Also, if you don't fully get something, seeing it visually can help you comprehend more. In addition, drawing out your points visually is helpful because if you can't articulate and make your points clear visually then it's probably not a good idea. Sharing through visual diagrams is a good way to vet an idea, explain it, and see its true merits." Lastly, Sam had a good sense of humor on why drawing out ideas is good for listening and understanding. Sam said, "By drawing things out you may be wrong, but you know for sure you're not confused." This is very good insight. It reminds me of a wise saying about how to ensure someone really understands and retains the message you are trying to convey. It is a Chinese proverb that goes like this,

> *"Tell me and I'll forget; show me and I may remember; involve me and I'll understand."*

Charles Whyte, Senior Director at Western Digital, had a refreshing approach to getting others to listen to you. Charles noted, "You need to earn respect. And you need to show competence for others to listen to you." This is very sensible. People listen to those they respect. And people respect those they believe are competent. What if you have these two things going for you, but people still do not listen to you? Charles has a fun solution. He stated, "Sometimes if you are talking and people are distracted and not listening just stop talking. Pause and stare. Wait for their attention. You will make your point very clear and command their respect and attention."

Lastly, getting others to listen to you is really about setting up the right environment for good listening. All the executives favored one-on-one meetings and face-to-face interactions as the most optimal means for effective communication. Then communicating effectively is paramount. The executives agreed that showing respect, listening to others intently first, asking questions, repeating back what you are hearing to confirm understanding, and taking notes all produce the best environment for listening and dialog. Additionally, Kevin Conley, SVP and GM at SanDisk, noted, "Share all openly and transparently. Have good lines of communication. Show good will." By doing all of the above you can hone a keen ability to get others to listen to you and create the right environment for great communication. This will truly help you be more successful in all you do!

"I only wish I could find an institute that teaches people how to listen. Business people need to listen at least as much as they need to talk. Too many people fail to realize that real communication goes in both directions."

—Lee Iacocca

Executive Corner

- Are you the type of person who makes it easy for others to listen and be open to your ideas?

- Be a person of real substance and good character who gives real value. Then people will genuinely like you, respect you, and be open to listening to you.

- Understand the needs of others and be able to communicate something that addresses their wants. Bring new and insightful information and people will listen.

Part Three:
The Heart of Success in...

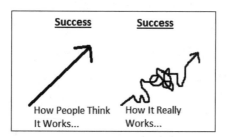

In this section of the book I share with you *The Heart of Success* in three different areas. I will identify the characteristics that make up successful people, what makes products succeed, and the ingredients that help create a successful career.

As this cartoon picture portrays, sometimes success looks different than we imagine. To bring it all home, take a minute to think about this anonymous quote:

"The road to success is not straight. There is a curb called Failure; a loop called Confusion; speed bumps called Friends; red lights called Enemies; caution lights called Family. You will have flats called Jobs. But, if you have a spare called Determination, an engine called

Perseverance, and insurance called Faith, you will make
it to a place called Success!"

Much of the information shared in this section about what makes successful people, products, and careers is common sense. However, it's the implementation of the knowledge shared that makes all the difference. This section will help you better understand success as it relates to these three areas and will give you the advice needed to take action that will lead you to greater success!

Chapter 4.
Successful People

"Success is not the key to happiness. Happiness is the key to success. If you love what you are doing, you will be successful."

—Albert Schweitzer

In this chapter we are looking into the hearts of successful people. I start with this quote by Albert Schweitzer because all the executives agreed upon one premise for being successful: *Love what you do.* You have to love what you do because that is what will drive you. Enjoying what you do is the fuel that ignites good work ethic, keeps you motivated, and keeps you passionate to persevere in all you do. Loving what you do will get you up in the morning and allow you to enjoy your day. Plus the biggest bonus is what Confucius says:

> *"Choose a job you love and you will never have to work a day in your life."*

When you love what you are doing your job feels more like play. It is important you do the things you sincerely enjoy because it is foundational to your joy, happiness, and ability to optimally sustain your success everything in your life.

Carlos Gonzalez, Senior Director at SanDisk, made this very direct but simple statement: "Make sure you are doing something you enjoy. You only go around this place once." Yes, we only live once and our time is precious. This seems obvious, but we sometimes take it for granted. If you're going to be spending ten hours or more of your day working, it seems only sane to do things you enjoy. You were created to utilize your inert talents and share them with the world. So nourish your natural gifts and bring them forward to shine uniquely and brightly. Carlos concluded with this point: "Be happy and passionate about what you do. People will follow and success will stem from that."

The advice from Carlos reminds me of my days as a Product Marketing Manager at Creative Labs. I was working on a project that introduced the worlds' first music keyboard and PC keyboard All-In-One product. As a musician and composer, I loved this project and poured my heart and soul into it. I spent my days going around the office getting people excited about the project, celebrating the sales momentum, and supporting my co-workers with any opportunities that came to light. At one point the brand manager said, "Keith, your enthusiasm is contagious."

The product was a success winning Creative Labs business in new retail channels like QVC TV and winning awards like "Best of CES" that year. The point is we are all influenced by the emotional states of the people we interact with. In the presence of cheerful, sincerely kind, upbeat people, we find it easier to become more cheerful and positive. Because the state of enthusiasm is contagious, if you want to increase your own level of enthusiasm, be around other people who are enthusiastic. Even talking to an enthusiastic person for a few minutes is frequently sufficient to elevate our own state. Think about how you can apply being passionate and positive in your own work. It can help be the one small change that makes a big difference!

Sam Nicolino, President and CEO of Adaptive Sound Technologies, commented on doing what you love with a similar point. Sam noted, "Do what you really like. Don't chase money or fads. Follow your heart." This really boils down to the simple phrase of wisdom you may have heard: "Do what you love and the money will follow." Matt Kaufman, President of CrunchBase, substantiated this point when he said, "Love what you do. Be passionate about your work. You need this to feel fulfillment and purpose in what you do. This will help you push through the hard time, setbacks, and deal productively with all the ups and downs." This is true.

Think about the example of Thomas Edison. Mr. Edison loved to invent things and create new innovations that helped mankind. This was his passion. This is why he never gave up and persisted on seeing a light bulb finally work despite many setbacks. He did not work on innovations just for money. It was what he wanted to do and he looked forward to working as part of his love for innovation. When meeting failures along the way, he did not give up. His love for his work and purpose pushed him forward. And when he did fail he counted it as one step closer to his destination. His passion helped him keep a positive outlook on all. This is why when asked about how many times he failed in trying to make a light bulb, Edison replied,

"I have not failed. I've just found 10,000 ways that won't work."

The point is, by loving what you do you're going to be able to weather the obstacles endured in your work life and be fueled to overcome adversity to march on towards greater success.

Loving what you do will also help you be passionate and enthusiastic. When Dick Sanquini, Chairman of PixelWorks, was asked how you can be successful he noted, "Enjoy what you do. Stay positive and good things will happen." It's pretty clear. When you love what you do, you're going to be happy and positive. And people like being around positive people, so by default you're going to be more involved with others and attract more opportunities.

Harry Dickinson, CEO of Fission Stream Technologies, said on this same logic pattern, "Love what you are doing. Have passion. Do things because you want to." This is good to reflect on. When you do things because you "want to" versus "have to" it brings an additional level of commitment and quality to your efforts. When you really want to do something you will deliver and see it through. This helps you be determined and persevere. Perseverance to march on against adversity is the fundamental trait to all successful people. When you love what you do and are passionate about it, you're going to want to do it. This enables better efforts and produces higher quality work that ultimately delivers better results. Toby Preston, Senior Director of Sales at Qualcomm, backed this up with this great motto: "Be passionate, enjoy it, live it, be it, and do it!" This is the theme of success that the company Nike promotes in their tagline which everyone seems to embrace: "Just Do It!"

A different key to being a successful person is developing your own high quality brand and getting along well with others. Your brand is your promise to others. The brand of YOU is what others come to see, expect, and believe about you. Separate from all your correspondence. Dick Sanquini, Chairman of PixelWorks, offered a great point that helps you deliver on your brand promise. Dick said, "Be very good and careful at setting expectations so you can always deliver results. Strive to under promise and over deliver. You always want to meet or exceed expectations. Be realistic when communicating to others on what you can do and offer." In short, you want to be the type of person who does what he says he is going to do. Be the person who others come to have faith in and trust to deliver on what is promised. Dick Sanquini hit this point home when I asked him for one tip to being successful. He said, "Set the right expectations then perform and deliver. Meet your commitments."

Another point that helps you deliver a good brand and

helps you conduct yourself well with others was noted by Russell Brady, Director of Corporate Communications at Adobe. Russell suggested, "Pay attention to the details. The devil is really in the details. Make sure you know them and then don't be afraid to correct someone if they make a mistake and you know you are right on the correction. Stand up for yourself if need be."

One time, Russell corrected Steve Jobs at Apple Computers in an email on a detail that Steve got wrong. Steve did not like that he had been corrected, so he called Russell into his office. As Russell made his way to Steve's office during a long walk from one end of the Apple corporate campus to the other he had a lot of time to think and was nervous about the correction and how Steve was going to react. When he got to Steve's office, sure enough, Steve was upset and called Russell out on that correction and accused Russell of being wrong. Russell stood his ground. Steve then picked up the phone to make a call to another executive to fact check and prove his point. After a chat with another source and a long awkward silence, Steve put the phone down and looked up at Russell. To Steve's surprise he was wrong on that detail and Russell was right with his correction. The moral of the story: Know the details and then don't be afraid to correct someone if they make a mistake and you know you are right. Even if that person is a bigwig executive, stand up for yourself and for what is right, when appropriate. In addition, know when it is necessary to issue a correction and when not. Proving that you are right isn't always the best course of action.

Another unique trait on being a successful person that resonated with all the executives is the importance of being your true self. Russell spoke at length on this point, suggesting, "Be yourself. Be your own person and character. Know where you stand on issues and don't mince words. Be direct with people. Have your own point of view. Think things through and have a substantial answer with prepared reasons on why you believe what you believe." This is important because it helps you be the authentic and unique person you are, a person who adds value in ways only you can. As Oscar Wilde said, "Be yourself, everyone else is already taken." Judy Garland said the same thing in a creative way too:

> *"Always be a first-rate version of yourself, instead of a second-rate version of somebody else."*

On another note, if you want to be a successful person all the executives said you need to be confident. You need to have the confidence to put yourself out there and to not be afraid. This allows you to do the other key aspect to being successful, and that is to take risks. Be willing to take calculated, well-thought-out, intelligent risks. You need to have the confidence that allows you to be bold and take a risk once you vetted things through and things seem worth a leap of faith. This allows you to pursue new opportunities and be open to new roles, tasks, and jobs that may require you to stretch yourself. It's by taking on new opportunities and stretching yourself that you gain valuable learning experiences and build more confidence. All of this leads to new leaps forward that can bring bigger rewards in your life.

Along the lines of confidence, another important

success trait was offered up by Mark Adams, President of Micron Technologies. Mark suggested the following as one of his top contributors to success: "You need to have that drive and want to compete. It's kind of like sports. You need that ability to compete, take on challenges, and want to win. Then you need the discipline necessary to do the hard work and do the right things to perform well and deliver results." All the executives backed up this point of needing to be driven, proactive, and a self-starter. You need to have that passion so it fuels all you do and helps you operate at peak performance. This is why the sports analogy to business is so relevant. Like a star athlete who gets up early, trains, eats well, and takes care of his mind, body, and spirit for peak performance, you must do the same as a businessperson if you want to see results. If you have important business meetings lined up, make sure you do the right preparations before and take care of yourself to look and feel great so you can deliver your best performance.

Many of the executives also suggested that to be a

successful person you need to have "Vision." Joe Castillo, GM at Acer, noted the following as one of his top contributors: "You need to understand top down what you are getting into. You must see the big picture and long-term view. Like a chess player, see moves ahead. Then have a methodical approach to moving forward. Be disciplined and think things through."

When I asked Craig McHugh, CEO of Cambridge SoundWorks, why some people succeed in Silicon Valley while others do not, his response was very similar. He noted, "People who are most successful in Silicon Valley are forward looking. They know how to see, plan, and execute two to three quarters down the road. To be successful you need to be like a chess player. See and be ready for two to three moves down the game. Always be thinking ahead." Think of the great leaders and visionaries like Steve Jobs and Bill Gates. They were looking ahead decades down the road when they saw the computer industry taking off way before its time. Even the great business leader, Thomas Watson, President of IBM in 1943, missed this vision when he said, "I think there is a world market for maybe five computers." The glaring lesson here is to make sure you take your head out of the sand. Look down the road and strive to have a vision of what is coming. Look around at the trends, new companies, and technologies in the works. Then connect the dots. What do you see? That is your vision!

To be most successful and secure the senior roles at companies, it's imperative to be someone who knows how to see the 10,000-foot perspective and connect the dots on how this affects your business. In addition, be future-looking so you have a clear understanding of what is coming down the pike and then take action to have your company ready to meet the opportunities and challenges ahead. Carlos Gonzalez, Senior Director at SanDisk, provided a great quote that helps tie this point together. He noted this Japanese proverb, "Vision without action is a daydream. Action without vision is a nightmare." This proverb provides a simple truth. You need both vision and then the action to move forward correctly to seize what lies ahead. Vision and taking action go hand-in-hand, like two wings of a dove that work together to elevate one up toward the heavens.

A special piece to being a successful person comes down to your relationships, people skills, and ability to network. You will be surprised how relationships you make at one company will lead to future opportunities down the road as people move on. Joe Weber, Global Director of Product Line Management at NeoPhotonics Corporation, listed "having a good network of relationships" as one of his top three contributors to success. Joe noted, "Make an effort to develop good relationships. You find in your career that good working relationships made at one company will often lead to your next opportunity at another company. For example, by giving a good sales training presentation and making a good impression on the people you work with in the present, years later will be remembered and can lead to your next job by the very same people you trained years prior."

Toby Preston, Senior Director of Sales at Qualcomm, advised similarly on the importance of your relationships.

Toby suggested, "Form a good network. Build relationships with leaders you believe in and can trust. Then listen to them. People who succeed have good mentors they
can trust and are associated with. It's also good to build a
good peer network so you can share and bounce ideas off
to solidify your concepts and build support."

One general rule on having good relationships comes
down to one simple thing: Be nice. Be a likeable person.
No one likes someone who is mean, disrespectful, and
unkind. As Abe Lincoln said, "A drop of honey catches
more flies than a gallon of gal." We have all seen people
at work be rude and uncaring. They may hold some high
positions and get by temporarily, but ultimately every
person they cross will remember how they made them
feel. The people they hurt may not say anything at the
time, but they will hold on to it and it will hinder that
relationship. Just be a good person. Genuinely care about
others and have good intentions in all you do. When you
are disrespected, address it in a kind way and take the
high road. It may be hard at times to bite your tongue,

but it will always be good for you at the end of the day to be nice and the better person. You can always look in the mirror with your head held high and know you made relationships important.

Lastly, being a successful person at the end of the day can be boiled down to the fundamental element of hard work. As Harry Dickinson, CEO of Fission Stream Technologies, noted, "A top contributor to your success is the willingness to roll up your sleeves and get the job done. Having the drive and being proactive." One acronym that is said frequently at Silicon Valley start-ups is "GID," which stands for "Get It Done." At a start-up you have to wear many hats. You may be selling one day, creating marketing messaging the next, and then shipping out a package that evening. To succeed you must be able to get your hands dirty and get the job done. No excuses. In addition, you need that drive and proactive nature to get things done on your own. All of this grows from your ability to work hard. When you work hard, two good things happen. First, you deliver your best results. Second, you open up more opportunities. If you're not working hard, you are missing opportunities. As Thomas Edison said,

> *"Opportunity is missed by most people because it is dressed in overalls and looks like work."*

All the advice and wisdom shared in this book can help you be successful, but working hard is the fuel that ultimately moves your train up the tracks. In summary, Joe Weber, Senior Director of Product Line Management at NeoPhotonics, said, "To succeed you need to be focused, driven, and be willing to work hard." This point is hit home by Joe Castillo, GM of Acer, "Be willing to put in the effort. Offer up the blood, sweat, toil, and tears to get the job done!" Overall, it's your hard work that will make you deliver quality, show people your passion and drive, and help you feel great about yourself, which all leads you to success. People can see how much you care by how hard you try. You can't fake good hard work and effort. People will recognize this in you, and applaud you.

My brother Jeff raised a good point about working hard and how it makes all the difference to your success.

He shared the temperature of boiling water analogy to illustrate his point. The point is as follows:

- At 211 degrees, water is hot. At 212, it boils.
- With boiling water comes steam. And steam can power a locomotive.
- And... it's that one extra degree that makes all the difference!

I will conclude this section with what Mark Adams, President of Micron Technologies, said when asked for concluding thoughts on succeeding in Silicon Valley: "Focus on your work ethic. Do good work and give good performance. Performance matters. Execution matters. You must deliver great results. So be results-orientated and have the discipline to do what is needed to get the job done well."

"When I was younger, I thought that the key to success was just hard work. But the real foundation is faith. Faith – the idea that 'I can do it' – is the opposite of fear ('What if I fail?'). And faith creates motivation which in turn leads to commitment, hard work, preparation ... and eventually success."

—Howard Twilley

Executive Corner

- Do you love what you do and have passion for your work? When your passionate about what you do people will follow and success will stem from that.

- Strive to under promise and over deliver. You always want to meet or exceed expectations.

- Be like a chess player. See and be ready for two to three moves down the game. Always be thinking ahead.

Sucess Story

Toby Preston, Senior Director of Sales at Qualcomm, said one of the top contributors to his success in Silicon Valley was forming a good network of leaders he believes in and trusts. Most importantly, he listens to these people and absorbs the information they share. Toby noted that you need to be open to others' ideas and be flexible enough to morph ideas into ways that help your personal development.

Toby shared an experience with a valuable mentor named Grant Ridgley who worked with him at Anthem Electronics. Grant taught Toby the importance of looking inside yourself and doing an honest assessment of where you are at, asking yourself questions like, "Are you fully applying yourself? Are you where you want to be? Are you giving it your all? Are you meeting your potential?"

One day Toby had a conversation with Grant, who candidly asked, "Toby, you are like a 700 hitter batting 120. What's up?" At this point, Toby was just getting by in his job and he was operating below 100 percent. This one single point and question, while spoken with sincere care and from a place of support, really struck Toby to the core and made a lasting impression. This was the first time someone professionally had gone out of his way to be blunt, direct, and give guidance to Toby. The ultimate value this moment had for Toby was an awakening and a change. He knew moving forward he had to do more and make more of himself. Toby did start applying himself and enjoyed greater success moving forward.

Bottom line: Confronting yourself with questions that force you to do an honest assessment of yourself brings forth a fundamental element of success. Make sure you are applying yourself and giving your best efforts in all you do. This trait can be the difference between succeeding and being just average. To succeed you must stretch yourself. Be passionate. Be confident and bold. Be willing to put yourself out there and give it all you got. Do this and you will tap into your fullest potential

Chapter 5.
Successful Products

"If you keep your eye on the profit, you're going to skimp on the product. But if you focus on making really great products, then the profits will follow."

—Steve Jobs

In this chapter we look into the heart of successful products. This quote is a great way to launch this chapter because it comes from one of the best visionary leaders to ever grace Silicon Valley. Under Steve Jobs' direction, Apple created some of the world's most successful products like the iPod, iPhone, and Mac computer. In addition, this quote from Steve Jobs makes a very poignant point about successful products. You must focus your time, resources, and talent first on making an amazing product. When you deliver a great product that offers new and innovative value to people, the money will follow. You can literally have a line of people wanting your products, as made famous by the lines out the door of Apple stores whenever a new iPhone is launched.

To make a product successful, you need a fantastic product and one that is differentiated. What then makes a fantastic product ultimately successful is one that delivers real value to a person. You know you are offering real value to someone when they enjoy the product so much they give up their resources for it. This could be giving up precious time to engage in the product (as people do creating Facebook accounts and using them daily) or giving up one's hard earned dollars to buy a new iPhone. You know you are also delivering real value when people not only give up their precious resources for it, but also encourage others to do the same. Then you have hit a home run!

However, it does not start with just having an amazing product nor does it necessarily end after you do deliver a great product. To have the best chance of success with your product you need to ensure that there is a market for it and that demand exists. Your safest bet is creating a fantastic product you know will have strong demand and will be playing in a large market with many potential customers. Once you have a great product that plays into a big market that has strong demand, it comes down to your ability to really deliver the product and scale up accordingly. The level of success your product is able to achieve will be based on other important factors. The other important factors come down to what MBA programs teach as the "5 P's of marketing." There are a few variations of the 5 P's of marketing, but the most common framework taught is: Product, Positioning, Placement, Pricing, and Promotion. The best way to learn about the 5 P's is to take a college course or read a book dedicated to the subject. Alternately, you can get the general framework through a search online. However, to save you time, here is the bottom line bulleted out. Read it slowly.

- First, you need to have a great product that plays in a big market with strong demand. There are some books that would differ with this statement because a lot of times a great product creates a market that didn't exist before. This is known as a blue ocean strategy or going after green field markets. While this is true, your highest chance for product success will come from serving a market that already exists.

- Secondly, take your great product and add in the right marketing actions to ensure it stands out from all the competing products and rises above to shine bright so customers see your product, understand what it has to offer, and are compelled to give up their money or resources for it.

- Thirdly, target the right people who are willing and ready to use your product. Ensure your product is in the right place for this target market to easily access it. Make sure you have the right messaging and content around the product so it's easy for people to understand the value and grasp all the wonderful things it will do for them.

- Fourthly, have the right price or value equation so it presents a good deal for customers' money or time. Make sure it's priced competitively compared to alternatives in the market. Employ good promotions around the product to raise awareness and give additional reasons for people to buy it, like special offers.

- Lastly, deliver on the thing that is most important to begin with. Deliver a great product ensuring the customers' experience is excellent and one they will recommend to their friends and be on board with buying again.

That is an example of the 5 P's of marketing summarized. This mix working together on all cylinders is the winning combination to your product succeeding.

Another important aspect of having a successful product was raised by Russell Brady, Director of Corporate Communications at Adobe. He noted that "Timing is everything."Russell shared the example of the Apple Newton. It was really the first iPhone or tablet-like device when it came out in the 90's, but it failed. Why? Because the market and infrastructure were not ready for the product so it was not well received. It was a great product, but that was not enough. What you need to have in addition to a great product is the right time, right place, and right infrastructure. Craig McHugh, CEO of Cambridge SoundWorks, substantiated this point. Craig noted, "You need to deliver a great product to the right market at the right time. The key is being able to accurately identify and target what the market will need months down the road. Being a good visionary and having a good pulse on the market is critical to products succeeding." For example, think of the iPod phenomena. This product took off and became wildly successful only after the digital music revolution began with audio files flooding the marketplace and other MP3 players already selling in stores. Apple saw the market opportunity and had a vision on what could be done better. They launched the iPod and even though it was late to the party, it was a superior product in design and function. In addition, it had great product marketing behind it making the iPod a cool, hip, and desirable audio player. Then Apple launched the iTunes music service providing a full ecosystem to access a music catalog instantly on the iPod in an easy, high quality way and the rest was history. Apple went from no market share to being the number one digital audio company in less than twenty months.

Overall, you have to have the right market variables

at play which can serve as a tailwind behind your back pushing your fantastic product forward towards success. Remember, you need the right product at the right time to the right market!

Harry Dickinson, CEO of Fission Stream Technologies, offered another good point on what is needed to make products succeed. One of his main points was ensuring your product is really built to what is needed by the marketplace. Observe what the market really wants and needs and then cater your product to serve that demand. Understanding the pain points of the customer and providing solutions that address these pain points is critical.

In Silicon Valley it's important to know the difference between being technically driven and market driven. Harry noted one reason products fail is because stuff is done by technologists who may do things just for the sake of technology. Starting things just to build a better mouse trap because it can be done when there is no market need or true demand is a losing proposition. To be successful when building a new product, ask yourself,

"Will the dog eat the dog food?" By being market driven you put the needs of the market and pain points of the customer first. Then build a product that delivers value to this market using technology as a means to an end. Joe Weber, Senior Director of Product Line Management at NeoPhotonics Corporation, substantiated upon this point on being market driven to have the best chance of success. Joe noted, "You need to be keen on listening to the market, customers, and know what the market will pay for your product. People get caught up in technology or their own idea of what people will buy instead of focusing on the real customer needs. You need a good vision of what the market wants and how you can impact lives with a product that people see value in that's worth them opening up their wallet for." In summary, once you really understand what the market wants and what specifically the customer needs, then create a product that offers a solution and delivers real value the customer will pay for. With that paradigm in place your product has the best chance of being successful.

Another good attribute to a product being successful is it being easy to use. Think of the big office superstore retailer Staples. What do their ads and commercials push in their messaging? The "Easy Button." Toby Preston, Senior Director of Sales at Qualcomm, really drove this point home. When asked why some products succeed while others fail, Toby said, "Simplicity! Think about solutions that bring value and are intuitive and easy to use. Ensure you solve real problems with simple easy solutions." If you think about some of the products you really enjoy, I'm sure one of the important elements is that it's so simple and easy to use. It's a no-brainer product that just seems to work. It's intuitive.

Dick Sanquini, Chairman of PixelWorks, summarized what makes a product successful and consolidated the points shared thus far. Dick said, "Products that succeed solve a real need. They address a big growing market with real demand. They have the right innovative technology with the right partnerships to deliver something valuable and accessible to all at the right price with the right features and benefits."

Lastly, all the executives agreed on one main point that can be the difference between the product succeeding and failing: The importance of having great marketing to support your product. Marketing helps put your product on a pedestal and makes it look, sound, feel, and appear amazing. Perception is king. Marketing is so powerful to making a product differentiated and desirable. If you ever wonder if marketing is important or want a good quote that shows you how marketing changes perception, remember this:

"Marketing is the difference between a greasy dead bird and finger-licking good!"

Kentucky Fried Chicken's marketing made this quote possible and really demonstrates how marketing makes a big difference.

You can look at the history of successful consumer products and note that many times they were not always the better product. Often they were the inferior technology and/or were lacking features compared to other competitive products available. Check out the famous case studies between Betamax and VHS or Blu-Ray versus HD-DVD. These were fierce battles over formats and products. What made the winning difference between which one was ultimately victorious was the marketing that helped provide a better solution and way to enjoy the product. In addition, the marketing created more awareness and demand for the product through alliances and with partners. And lastly, the overall marketing mix was executed on shifting customers to favor a specific format and product. Bottom line: A good product needs good marketing. Marketing can be the difference between a premiere brand in first place and the cluster of runners-up. Don't have marketing be an afterthought. Make sure it is a priority and get everyone involved to make it a very important part of your product's success. As David Packard said,

> *"Marketing is too important to be left to the marketing department."*

Overall, having a successful product connects back to what we have been defining as success for you personally and professionally. It's all about doing the right things, for the right reasons, and in the right way to deliver something that makes a difference. Aim to bring greater happiness, joy, and contentment with any product you work on. Have this product offer a good whole hearted experience and be of quality and value.

"When you're a carpenter making a beautiful chest of drawers, you're not going to use a piece of plywood on the back, even though it faces the wall and nobody will see it. You'll know it's there, so you're going to use a beautiful piece of wood on the back. For you to sleep well at night, the aesthetic, the quality, has to be carried all the way through."

—**Steve Jobs**

 Executive Corner

- Are you making something fantastic that is really needed and delivers real value?

- Make sure you deliver your offering to the right market at the right time.

- Put in great marketing to ensure your great product stands out and gets known.

Chapter 6.
Successful Careers

"Communication – the human connection – is the key to personal and career success."

—Paul J. Meyer

Having a successful career is all about working with good people, being with good companies, having good work-life balance, being compensated well for the value you deliver, and advancing your career in wise ways that are part of a plan. As the beginning quote presents, being a great communicator and having excellent interpersonal relationship skills are vital. These skills will empower you to connect and build good relationships with people and influence them. This is the tailwind at your back that helps push your career forward.

Being a strong communicator and good listener is first and foremost. Throughout my career I have seen how giving good presentations and knowing how to read the room and listen to others makes a big difference. Also, speaking up in meetings with valuable contributions and communicating clearly is key to advancing your career. There are plenty of organizations you can join to help you be a great public speaker and learn how to be good with people in various settings. For example, Toastmasters International is an excellent group that can help you improve your public speaking skills and interactions with others. I recommend you find a local club and join.

In the executive interviews, when we talked about communication and its impact on a person's career,it was striking to hear them all emphasize the importance of how you communicate. Dick Sanquini, Chairman of PixelWorks, said his biggest tip to having a successful career was communicating in a way that sets the right expectations. Dick said, "Be very careful and good at setting expectations so you can always deliver results. Under promise and over deliver. You always want to meet or exceed expectations, so be realistic. Set the right expectations then perform, deliver, and meet your commitments."

Having good relationships and being able to connect personally with people is important to helping you succeed in your career. It's so paramount that Craig McHugh, CEO of Cambridge SoundWorks, listed having good relationships as his number one tip in having a successful career in Silicon Valley. Craig recommended, "Create a strong network of relationships with good people. Be proactive and seek out relationships. Join organizations, groups, and network. Work with and surround yourself with great people, learn and grow from each other. Bring real value to others and help elevate them too." There are many organizations that help foster this networking. Think of joining your alumni association or forums like the Churchill or Rotary Club.

One of the key themes shared by the executives was working hard and delivering real value to the organization. You want to be able to show real results that grow the business. When you produce real results things tend to fall into place. Carlos Gonzalez, Senior Director at SanDisk, really emphasized this point. He noted,

"Companies want to take advantage of good talented people and their capability to move the needle. The company will ask them to take on more responsibility as they see the hard work, value, and results delivered by the individual. Focus on adding value to your company in areas that are important to the business. Contribute good value to areas the company is focused on." One strategic career move tip is to align yourself with a role that adds value to what the company considers its cash cow or most important new growth area. For example, if you work at Intel, ensuring you have a role in engineering that works on the next generation of new chips powering the next wave of electronics is a wise career move versus being stuck in a dying segment of the business.

Having a big picture and strategic view of the business was another prevalent thread of advice. Hugh Walker, VP at EMC, suggested, "Establish a broad perspective on the core fundamentals of the business. See the big picture. Understand the financials. The planning, P&L, and balance sheets." Carlos Gonzalez from SanDisk backed this point up when he said, "Also, look at the big picture and think strategically. Get involved in helping to solve some of the bigger challenges of the company and do more than just whatever narrow slice you may be handed to do." Companies tend to reward those people who take on responsibility and offer up their time and talents. Everyone likes to see someone with initiative who throws his hat in the ring to contribute more. Always keep an eye out for ways you can add more value.

Becoming really competent in a special area of expertise was another common theme among the executives. Charles Whyte, Senior Director at Western Digital, suggested, "Focus on something and be an expert. Get competence. This will help you gain confidence and build respect. You can get trust and respect by showing people you know your stuff and deliver good work. Getting a good education and training can also be helpful to building your competency." Matt Kaufman, President of CrunchBase, gave his take on the importance of having competency to boost your career. Matt suggested, "You need to form a solid foundation of skills, experience, expertise, and knowledge. You have to get real experience and take the time to put in the effort to establish this base. It's kind of like sports and being a biking athlete. You need that base of thousands of miles of training. You need to ride all those miles to build up your strength and foundation. Work on your biking, get the depth, and then you can draw from it."

One of the key traits to a successful career that is directly related to your personal success is the theme of working hard. As Joe Castillo, GM at Acer Computers, stated, "Driven people that are motivated and willing to put in the effort are the winners. You got to be willing to put in the time and effort. Work hard to deliver results and earn your title versus 'hired in.' Bleed your company color!" This concept of bleeding your company color is a powerful one. It's all about showing dedication, hard work, and loyalty to the company you work for. Joe elaborated on this point further, noting,"It's also about treating the company's money as if it's your own." This is a great tip. If you treat your company resources like they are your own assets, then you know you always have your company's best interest at heart, which helps you deliver the right quality, and ethical work.

Another common piece of advice for advancing your career was the opportunity that is afforded by getting in with small companies. Many times, working for start-ups was the pivotal moment to these executives in achieving leap frog career growth and gaining the executive title stripes. When you work at smaller companies you can assume bigger titles, get more responsibility, and rise when they grow. In addition, you can meet a lot of great people along the way. Sam Nicolino, President and CEO of Adaptive Sound Technologies, elevated this point further. Sam recommended, "To advance your career, think about putting your own money into something. Start your own company. Take chances, risks, and be open to new jobs and career transitions." Think about it. There is no quicker way to getting your "President and CEO" title than by starting your own company. The second fastest way to advance your career and secure a higher title is to join small companies that are more flexible about giving bigger titles and offer great room for growth.

When it comes to advancing your career, at some point your job title becomes important. Getting your "stripes" (meaning the Director title or above) at a company helps validate your expertise, experience, and management capability. Additionally, the higher title you assume usually comes with more responsibility and bigger compensation. As alluded to earlier,one advice point from the executives was to work for smaller companies like start-ups versus big corporations. One of the reasons for working with a start-up is it can help you secure the bigger title sooner rather than later. Getting a Director or above title at a 30,000 plus person global company is harder to claim than at a start-up of thirty employees. The big corporate office politics can also make it more challenging to climb up the ranks, whereas with a start-up company climbing the ranks can happen more quickly because a start-up often grows at a faster clip and adds new hires after you're in which can elevate your position. In addition, you get to expand with the company as it grows so your title has an opportunity to elevate faster via this means too. Lastly, your job title growth is important to demonstrating you are advancing in your career. However, people who concentrate only on titles may miss the importance of driving value for the company. Make sure you are creating value first and foremost. The key is gaining the experience that supports the title. The bigger title will follow.

Advancing your career is also about picking the right companies to work for. You want to pick winning corporations to join. Look to join companies that are growing well, have a healthy business with many opportunities to leverage, and employ smart people. The executives suggested the importance of working with smart people. Go where you know you have intelligent people to engage with because you will learn and gain very valuable experiences from that to help you grow. In addition, you will make many good relationships that add to your overall network value that can be helpful in the future too.

Another point the executives emphasized is knowing when to stay, and,most importantly, when to move on from a company. If you are not sensing growth at your company, or feel you are not surrounded by smart experts, or feel the company is on a downward slope and nothing you do can really make a difference, then consider letting go and moving on to a new company. One way to have a good career is to always be positioned with a good company serving a good market.

Lastly, Mark Adams, President of Micron Technologies, said something that ties all this career advice together. When I asked Mark his number one tip for having a successful career in Silicon Valley, he said, "It all comes down to having a plan, then executing on this plan you establish. You have to have a game plan and then aggressively go after it. Put the right pieces and efforts in place to execute and achieve your plan's aims." This is excellent advice because to advance your career you should have a well-thought-out plan on what your aims are and where you want to be, with documented steps that are necessary to achieve your plan. Lewis Carroll, an English writer, mathematician, logician, Anglican deacon, and photographer once said,

> *"If you don't know where you are going, any road will take you there."*

The point of that wisdom is you always need to have a plan! In addition, Mark suggested the following good advice on building your career that is really the icing on the cake: "Invest your time in a company and give loyalty. Stay long enough to establish a good legacy at the companies you work for. You always want to be known as a big producer. "

"Concentration of effort and the habit of working with a definite chief aim are two of the essential factors in success which are always found together. One leads to the other."

—Napoleon Hill

Executive Corner

- Are you a great communicator and public speaker?

- Create a strong network of relationships with good people.

- Focus on adding value in areas that are important and contribute good value to people where it matters.

Success Story

Sam shared a fascinating story about his career path to becoming CEO of Adaptive Sound Technologies. The short version is as follows.

In the 1980's, Sam worked as an engineer with Intel, a leading tech company. By all accounts he had a great job and was comfortable and successful. However, Sam's passion was in the audio and processing world and he wanted to do his own chip design. Intel was not giving Sam the opportunity to do his own design, which hindered his ability to demonstrate leadership and get more responsibility. So after some deliberation, Sam took a risk. He left Intel. Sam left all that Intel stock, benefits, and perks behind because he wanted to further his career and have the opportunity to make his own processor. Sam went to another company, Atari Computers, which was doing OK but teetering a bit. At Atari, Sam got the opportunity to make his own audio processor and all seemed to be on track. Then Atari went out of business. Sam lost his job within twenty-four months after he joined.

You may be quick to say, "What a failure. It was a bad decision to leave Intel. Sam lost his job and left all those benefits behind. How could this be a good career move?" Here is the success lesson that emerged. What seemed like a setback led to one of Sam's best successes to date. Atari going out of business launched Sam as an entrepreneur — he was hired as a consultant to get the audio chip he created working for another company. This gave Sam the opportunity to found his own company. He hired a team to support his new company and it grew into a very successful business. Now, because of this path, Sam was able to launch Adaptive Sound Technologies Inc. The company now has the world's number one best-selling sleep machine product,which he created.

Bottom line: Because Sam took a risk and leap of faith to leave Intel it helped him find new success. Sam would not be where he is today as an entrepreneur and leader of a great company if it were not for taking steps to follow his passion and be open to new challenges. One of the top contributors to Sam's successful career in Silicon Valley was taking chances and building good bridges along the way. Sam also noted that you need to be open to new jobs and transitions. There is always an option to start your own company too. Sam said, "Do what you love. Do what you are excited about and success will follow. Even if that thing fails, you enjoyed doing it, and new doors open up." This quote made famous by Al Bernstein makes this point ring true, "Success is often the result of taking a misstep in the right direction."

Part Four:
The Extra Beat of Success...

In this section of the book I share some extra heart beats on success in four different areas. First is some perspective and advice on keeping good work-life balance. The second area includes insights on how you can learn from failure. The third offers tips to help you stay fresh and current in your career. And finally, the fourth area is a high level review on how faith may play a role in your success.

As this cartoon portrays, success takes continuous work. I hope these extra beats of success provide you additional wisdom and guidance to keep your success train moving down the tracks with full steam.

Chapter 7.
Work-Life Balance

"Work is a rubber ball. If you drop it, it will bounce back. The other four balls—family, health, friends, integrity—are made of glass. If you drop one of these, it will be irrevocably scuffed, nicked, perhaps even shattered."

—Gary Keller

I start this chapter on work-life balance with this quote because it hammers the point home that success in your job and career is nothing if your personal life is not a success too. To be a true success you need your personal life to be given the right time, nourishment, and quality care it deserves to enable you to fully flourish as a person. In sports terms, you need to be a pro both on and off the field. You need to get your ducks in a row with your personal life so you can bring your "A Game" to your professional life.

Life is bigger than just your job and making money. It's really about you being the best person you can be.

This means being a loving father, husband, wife, mother, brother, sister, son, daughter, and so for this important. You really want to be a great human being in all your personal relationships because if you get that right, the rest comes more easily professionally. Always make sure you are balanced as it relates to your professional and personal life. Be aware of your time and keep that optimal balance. To accomplish this balance it's crucial to remember what's most important in life. At the end of the day, the job, money, and career will fade. Only you and your personal life will remain. Keep that perspective in mind. My father once told me, "Keith, remember my words. Your friends will come and go. Your job will come and go, but your family will always be there for you and that is what really matters."

When interviewing the executives, I asked for advice on how to balance your work and personal life. It was fascinating to hear that the majority of executives struggle with finding the right work-life balance. Many of them humbly acknowledged that their work-life balance is not something they are really good at and admit it's an area that needs improvement. The executives confessing that work-life balance is something they struggle with is a good start. Acknowledging you have a problem is always the first step to solving it. I believe this is another good example of what makes someone truly successful. Part of the whole hearted success definition this book aims to give you is being humble enough to understand your weaknesses and then being driven enough to overcome them. It is understandable the executives struggle with this balance. They lead technology companies within a fiercely competitive sector of business,so they have many demands on their time. Most of them work way beyond the standard forty-hour work week. Despite this challenge, all the executives stressed the importance of a good work-life balance and offered up some great tips on keeping balance.

Sam Nicolino, President and CEO of Adaptive Sound Technologies,said this about keeping balance: "Make family a priority. Take time to be with your kids and go on vacations. Also, have something to take your mind off work like jogging, music, family, or whatever your hobbies are. Make sure you know yourself and know your limits. Know when to say 'No' to things professionally when things start becoming unbalanced. Sometimes the best thing for your work and performance is to take time off. Come back with fresh eyes and new ideas generated from your time away." Joe Weber, Global Director of Product Line Management at NeoPhotonics, elaborated on this point: "Maintain interests outside of work like family, church, music, and sports. Set priorities and goals for your personal life too, not just work. In short, you need to have a life outside of work." Joe made me laugh when he suggested, "You have to join the Get a Life club!"

The point of taking time off away from work being a good thing for your professional contributions was substantiated by Matt Kaufman, President of CrunchBase. Matt noted, "Understand and respect the importance of the creativity and good thinking that occurs outside of work when you are not at your desk. It is often a great time to ask employees to noodle on a question on a

Friday afternoon. Ask them to think about a challenge over the weekend. Some good answers can come back that Monday morning! Also, make efforts to schedule and organize your time to keep a good work-life balance. There are diminishing returns when sitting at your desk and being stuck in the office too long." Many people suggest keeping a calendar to track all of your obligations, both professionally for meetings and also personally for your time away with friends and family. Make sure you schedule in these other personal activities to ensure they are kept as a priority and keep your schedule clear so you can attend them.

Joe Castillo, GM of Acer, stated the importance of keeping your personal life in high priority especially when it comes to your family. Joe suggested, "Do your best to always be there for your family. Do the things you need to do for your personal life. Have discipline to schedule your workouts. Get on a red eye flight if that is what it takes to get home in time for a family soccer game. Schedule your vacations. Also, having a good loving spouse who is supportive can make all the difference." Amen to that! I once heard Jim Harbaugh, coach of the San Francisco 49ers, state in a press interview the importance of a supportive spouse. He said, "A happy wife is a happy life!" Russell Brady, Director of Corporate Communications at Adobe, noted in a similar vein, "Prioritize your family and put them number one. If your family is OK and happy, then you will be happy. Know when to unplug and shutdown to take well-needed breaks and get away from work."

A clear theme that emerged from all the executives on work-life balance was putting your family first. Craig McHugh, CEO of Cambridge SoundWorks, said this: "You must make family and your personal life a high priority. Everything you do is for the kids and family. Make sure you schedule your personal life and keep a balance. With the connected-device world we live in you can work from anywhere, anytime, so you can do your work around your personal schedule. For example, when at home with the kids and they go to study, you can then take time to catch up on your work things too." Some executives referred to this mixing of personal and work life as "life work blend" versus balance. I believe the key is to remember there is a time and place for everything. Keep a good healthy balance or "work life blend." Extremes of any kind are not sustainable. Slow and steady wins the race. You must stay balanced so your personal life can be taken care of and in turn your professional life can be taken care of too.

Consider your success in life and rising to your highest potential accomplished only when your personal life and professional life are well balanced and work together hand in hand. Imagine a white peaceful bird flying to the heavens with one wing flapping away from being the best person in your job and career. The other wing is flapping away based on your success in all you do personally. You need both wings working together in sync and balance to fly up to success in the best way.

How do you apply this lesson of ensuring your personal and professional life is balanced and working together? For starters, when you are at your job, give it all you got and deliver. When you are at home with your family, give them all your quality attention and time. Specifically, when you are on your vacation recognize it's your limited personal time. This means putting your phone, laptop, and other devices down when you're around family and friends so you can enjoy the quality time and depth of the moment with them. The job will always be there, but the people you are with at that moment may not be.

Kevin Conley, SVP and GM at SanDisk, had this advice on keeping a good work and personal life balance. "You must focus and prioritize. Your time goes to where you give your attention and focus. You need a priority system. Understand and distinguish that not everything is important. You need the ability to let some things go. Keep the right perspective. Make sure you take time to do what is good for you. For example, get your exercise and spend quality time with your family and friends. This can help you recharge and be a better employee and asset to your company." I personally have seen Kevin live his words — he focuses on planning out his day to achieve a healthy work-life balance. Kevin is able to lead SanDisk as an executive and still makes time to attend soccer games twice a week and socialize with others. Think about how you can prioritize your work and personal life too so all stays in balance.

Many of the executives emphasized the importance of health and fitness as a key driver to your personal life and overall success. Charles Whyte, Senior Director at Western Digital, substantiated the importance of making time to exercise during your personal time. Charles suggested," Prioritize health. That is the wealth of the wise. Your health comes first so schedule your fitness in. Push yourself to have good balance and succeed in all areas." Dick Sanquini, Chairman of PixelWorks, elaborated on the importance of your wellness in saying, "The most important thing is your health. Having good health holds back and slows down your degradation. Focus on these three things to keep healthy and well. First, get regular consistent sleep. Aim to get at least eight hours of rest every night. Secondly, exercise both aerobic and weight training consistently. And lastly, make sure you eat healthy consistently. Avoid big meals or bad foods. Rather, have a healthy lifestyle of eating the right foods and reasonable portions." I have come to understand a very simple way to achieve a healthy diet and good fitness. First, consider having the majority of your diet consist of water-rich foods. This can be any form of soups, salads, or vegetarian dishes. Second, get as much movement in your day as possible. From little ten-minute jogs or walks in the morning or a one-hour workout in the afternoon or evening. The point being is to move more than you sit. Motion is lotion for the joints. This will help you burn calories, boost energy, and keep well overall.

Another unique angle to your work-life balance is keeping your value system top of mind. Toby Preston, Senior Director of Sales at Qualcomm, made this point clear. "Have values and invest in your value system. Values can change over time so be flexible and adjust to them based on your timeline in life. Be able to shift and real-locate your time when necessary. Be willing to sacrifice your own agenda at times for the good of others. Be able to compromise. Overall, just strive for good balance in all things." Think about your life as having a path like a roll-ercoaster. There are many ups, downs, and winding trails throughout your journey. At certain points things take on different priorities so we need to know when to sacrifice and focus on the things that are most important at each step of our journey. For example, we go through phases from childhood to adulthood where different things mean more to us at different times. We have a time to be single, a time to be married, a time to be a student, a time to be a professional, a time to be a father or grandfather, and on it goes. The point is to know where you are in your life jour-ney and what your priorities are at each juncture along the way. This way you can make adjustments when necessary to give the right areas the right time and focus.

One visual tip to help you keep a good work-life bal-ance and prioritize your lifewith the right perspective is to imagine a pyramid. For example, Maslow's hierarchy of needs is often portrayed in the shape of a pyramid with the largest and most important needs at the bottom. The bottom portion of the pyramid would be your physiological needs like breathing, food, and water. Consider this Maslow's pyramid example, but change it with a perspective of prioritizing your life with the hierarchy of what's most important. Based on what I have learned from interviewing the executives your life should be ordered by what is most important as follows. First your faith, then your health and wellness, then aligning all of this with a focus on your family and friends, being a good person and citizen of the world, and then ultimately contributing this to your job and career. Here is a cartoon to visualize this concept of making sure you prioritize your life correctly.

The bottom line is to view the world and your life with the right "big picture" in mind. Know what is most important, then prioritize your time and focus to make the right decisions in alignment with this bigger perspective so you have the right work-life balance.

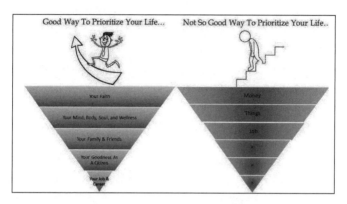

"Just as your car runs more smoothly and requires less energy to go faster and farther when the wheels are in perfect alignment, you perform better when your thoughts, feelings, emotions, goals, and values are in balance."

—Brian Tracy

Executive Corner

- Are you keeping a good, healthy work-life balance?

- Sometimes the best thing for your work and performance is to take time off.

- Take care of your health. Make a healthy lifestyle your first priority.

Chapter 8.
Learning from Failure

"Failure should be our teacher, not our undertaker. Failure is delay, not defeat. It is a temporary detour, not a dead end. Failure is something we can avoid only by saying nothing, doing nothing, and being nothing."

—Denis Waitley

Growth in life often comes from the wisdom gained from our failings. It is the mistakes along the way that give us the valuable learning experiences we need to grow and become smarter and more capable people. The key to making failures work for you is to recognize failure as a temporary defeat, a learning lesson, and an opportunity to bounce right back to become a better and stronger person as a result. In addition, it helps even more to learn from other people's failures so you don't have to make the same mistakes.

Everyone who has achieved great success in life has been through some failures. In fact, the most successful will all share the theme that, if you are not failing at points along your journey, then you are not taking enough risks. You are being too safe. You need to put yourself out there for an opportunity to shine and maximize your growth even if that means exposing yourself to a potential failure. It's through these risks that we grow the most. As Theodore Roosevelt so eloquently said,

> *"Far better is it to dare mighty things, to win glorious triumphs, even though checkered by failure... than to rank with those poor spirits who neither enjoy nor suffer much, because they live in a gray twilight that knows not victory nor defeat."*

The executives in this book all agree that failure is nothing to be feared, but rather to be embraced for the valuable learning lessons that come forth from these temporary setbacks. A quote by Mary Kay promotes this point well: "Every failure, obstacle, or hardship is an opportunity in disguise. Success in many cases is failure turned inside out."

I asked the executives if they have ever failed before and if they could offer any key lessons they gained. They were all quick to laugh and admit they have failed many times. At the same time they acknowledged great learning that sprouted from their mistakes and were eager to share. Here are some of the top learning lessons gained from some of the executives' failures.

- Failure teaches you that you must pick yourself up, be independent, and be a self-starter. Always be ready to try again and start over.

- Don't believe everything you're told. Often in business you can be spoon-fed a party line. Be open-minded, but also keep your level of skepticism so you can avoid being fooled. Trust, but verify. As some Silicon Valley lingo goes, "Be careful not to just drink the Kool Aid." If something does not seem true, then it may not be so and if something seems too good to be true then it probably is.

- Keep a healthy level of skepticism. It's OK to be opportunistic and positive overall, but be rational and realistic. Always be a good skeptic.

- Sales are all bull until the real money comes in the door. A purchase order or booking may look good, but the truth is in the pudding. When you actually get paid is when sales become real.

- Failure teaches you to never give up. Be persistent and do the hard work needed to fix issues.

- If you are not careful, expectations can run astray and unrealistic expectations can set in like weeds in a garden not manicured. Set the right expectations and be sure to manage expectations very well. Keep everyone on the same page and communicate well to set realistic expectations.

- Think long-term about sales growth and think thoughtfully about how you go about sales growth. One danger can be growing sales too fast and not growing sales in the right way. Then management expects the same sales growth and expectations become out of whack, especially if the sales growth did not come from healthy means.

- Make sure you are getting a 360-degree view of a situation so you understand all facets to make the best decisions. Also, understand the people that are involved in a project and how good they are so you have a full assessment of what the reality of the situation is. The people and team can make or break a decision and/or company result.

- Understand that failure is not a bad thing. Learn from your mistakes. Know that everyone makes mistakes. It's what you do when you fall down that makes all the difference. Get back up and fight on! As the Chinese proverb goes, "Fall seven times and stand up eight."

- Be careful of joining a start-up or small company if a recession is about to hit. Make sure you check a company's finances, run rate, balance sheet, and funding to ensure a solid footing is established before you make a leap of faith to join. Know the financial climate of the industry and financials of the company before making your final decision to join or not.

- Make sure you adequately prepare for the unexpected or other eventualities. Have a Plan B in case "What if..." happens!

- Always work for a company that you can relate to and be proud of. Identify companies who know who they are, have a clear vision with real value, a good culture, and offer a long-term opportunity.

- Don't shun people for making mistakes. Give them the opportunity to make it right. It's good to not point and blame. Allow people to recover and make amends.

- Report and provide status updates with an open and honest assessment. Give the truth of a situation. Provide all the good, bad, and the ugly.

Don't work off of wishful thinking. Make sure all is done and can be done with a realistic view.

- Be careful of what you sign up for. Make sure you vet problems out and do all your diligence on a situation up front before committing yourself.

- "Be a leader, not a follower."My father told me this quote. He would follow it up by asking me, "If your friend jumped off a bridge, would you?" In short, don't blindly follow the herd. The herd mentality can often lead you to slaughter. Be smart, awake, and keep your own eye out on the horizon. Go out into the world and blaze your own trail. As my brother Jeff likes to say, "If it is to be, it is up to me!"

- Lastly, always keep an open mind and seek out learning opportunities from failures. Sometimes things at one place may not work out, but it leads to new doors opening and new opportunities. When results don't come out the way you hoped, it is important to learn from the mistakes and ask yourself, "What did I not see? What did I miss?" You need to have a "learn from mistakes" approach and analyze everything so you can learn and make changes where needed. Figure out how mistakes happened so you can improve, learn from them, and make sure you do not make the same mistake twice. Move forward new and improved from past mistakes so you can keep getting better!

"Every adversity, every failure, every heartache carries with it the seed of an equal or greater benefit."

—Napoleon Hill

Executive Corner

- Are you afraid to fail?

- If you are not failing at points along your journey, then you are not taking enough risks.

- If you are going to take a risk, make sure it's a well-calculated one and prepare for the unexpected or other eventualities. Have a Plan B in case "What if…" happens.

Chapter 9.
Staying Fresh!

"A ship in port is safe,
but that's not what ships are built for."

—Rear Admiral Grace Murray Hopper

For you to be most successful it's important to always acquire wisdom, experience, and knowledge and to constantly hone your skills. To best succeed, you should be a lifelong learner. Strive to be a full-time student of life! This is the credo for staying fresh in your career and living a robust life. The key is to not get stuck in your ways. Don't be closed minded and get complacent. Complacency posts are the road blocks that hold you back from achieving your greatest success. Go ahead and take on challenges when the time is right. As Joshua J. Marine said,

"Challenges are what make life interesting; overcoming them is what makes life meaningful."

I asked the executives how to stay fresh and current to be

most effective in your career. Here are some of the themes they shared.

The first theme to staying fresh is to attend industry events, seminars, and forums so you are getting the latest information and ideas to help you become more knowledgeable. By attending conferences and trade shows you also have the opportunity to network and get more in the mix. Sam Nicolino, President and CEO of Adaptive Sound Technologies, stated, "Take advantage of workshops, trainings, seminars, and new books. Companies will offer these things so participate in them." Charles Whyte, Senior Director at Western Digital, provided similar feedback: "Attend forums, conferences, summits, and then make sure you network and socialize." This is an important point because it's one thing to attend a conference and it's another to get in the mix and talk with people. Don't be a wallflower. Socializing with people at the conference and building relationships is where you will benefit most.

A second theme from the executives was around keeping current on the financial industry. Harry Dickinson,

CEO of Fission Stream Technologies, said, "Read up on what the tech analysts and investment analysts are saying. They can tell you a lot. Also, follow the money to know what areas in business are hot and growing." Many of the executives suggested studying other companies, the stock market, and understanding what is moving within the financial industry so you are kept abreast of the economy as it relates to your job, career, and the company you work for too. This insight can help you with your career by ensuring you are not at a sinking ship company or working in an industry that is being disrupted. Keep alert and be on guard. Make changes to what you are doing and where you are working if need be.

A third theme was stretching yourself to ensure you keep learning. As Sam Nicolino, President and CEO of Adaptive Sound Technologies, said, "Go into new learning areas. Sometimes it can be uncomfortable, but do it anyways. Stretch yourself. Get out of your comfort zone." This hammers home the point to avoid complacency and to stay on the cutting edge of doing and learning. Hugh

Walker, VP at EMC, made this point as well: "Always be prepared to learn new things and be open, flexible, and adaptive to change. Be a lifelong learner. Look to be mentored and look into mentoring others as a way to grow too." I believe Toby Preston, Senior Director of Sales at Qualcomm, said it well in closing on this theme: "Get out of your cocoon. Extend yourself to new people and ideas. Get out there and mix it up with various people, products, ideas, and technology to keep learning!" I think this is where working for both big and small companies throughout your career can be helpful. By putting in some time at both you gain a fuller perspective of business plus acquire unique traits that only come from working within different size companies. Each one can serve you in an exceptional way. At a small company, you learn to wear many hats and just get things done by bootstrapping. At a large company, you learn how to be a valuable part of a big organization, weave successfully through politics, and make big things happen when you have bigger budgets and more time at your disposal.

Staying fresh also requires a certain mind-set and disposition. Matt Kaufman, President of CrunchBase, made this good point: "Realize you are always behind and never caught up. So motivate yourself to read and talk with others in the know like VCs [venture capitalists] who are always talking to people with the new ideas. Have an attitude that's very open to learn. There is no magic. It's hard to stay fresh. It takes time and effort. You have to work at it. So read and listen a lot."Keep your eyes open and alert to always learning new things.

Lastly, almost all the executives noted that you really need to stay in the mix and expose yourself to many conversations with lots of different people. As Joe Castillo, GM at Acer, suggests, "Have good relationships. Stay in contact with people and network. Stay in the information flow." It's important to be in touch with a variety of sources because it keeps you open to a plethora of unique ideas and information that can give you a colorful perspective on all the issues. Dick Sanquini, Chairman of PixelWorks, suggested, "Learn a lot in many areas. Get a broad skill set and high level, big picture view. Keep learning and putting yourself in new areas." By doing all of this you can stay current, relevant, and add more value to your company and the people around you. In short, stay in the know and stay fresh. Keep learning!

"Those people who develop the ability to continuously acquire new and better forms of knowledge that they can apply to their work and to their lives will be the movers and shakers in our society for the indefinite future."

—Brian Tracy

 Executive Corner

- Are you a life long learner?

- Attend industry events to keep in the know and network.

- Leaders are readers so keep abreast of industry news and keep engaged in the latest trends impacting your field.

Chapter 10.
Faith in Silicon Valley?

"It's faith in something and enthusiasm for something that makes life worth looking at."

—Oliver Wendell Holmes

When you look at having a successful life and career you may ask yourself,"Does faith matter?" Does having faith in your life make a difference to your success? This is a great question and one worth pondering. Perhaps you have thought about this before or even struggled with this aspect of your life. Admittedly,this is a sensitive topic and can be controversial. There are many different opinions. In fact I received a wide array of opinions on this subject from all the executives. I'm not here to convince you one way or another, but I felt that any book on success requires at least a genuine touch on the subject of faith. Whatever your position is on faith it is something worth thinking about deeply. It is my hope that the perspectives and executive feedback shared in this chapter — while presented consciously and neutrally at a high level — will be helpful to your discernment of how faith may play a role in your success.

First off, what is faith? Faith can mean believing in something bigger than yourself or a higher power that adds meaning and perspective to your life. Or faith can mean something more specific to you like believing in God and living out a specific religious world view. The challenging part with faith is it requires you to believe in something unseen or not 100 percent known or proven. That is the point of faith and why you're probably familiar with the phrase, "It takes a leap of faith..." Sometimes you just have to jump and trust. As Martin Luther King, Jr., so eloquently said,

> *"Faith is taking the first step even when you don't see the whole staircase."*

Sometimes faith is that little thing in your heart that tells you something despite proof or what you may fully know at the moment. As Khalil Gibran suggests, "Faith is a knowledge within the heart, beyond the reach of proof."

In short, having faith means you believe in something. For example, if you have faith in God it means you believe that God exists. This faith built upon your belief will result in how you view the world and live your life. In terms of fully understanding yourself and your life, one question to sincerely ask is,"What do you believe?" What do you really believe and how does this impact your perspective on life, your attitude, choices, conduct, and your overall character formation? We all believe in something so it's a matter of clearly understanding what this belief is and understanding how these beliefs are impacting who we are as a person. This book may be worth its weight in gold if you just take time to reflect upon this faith question and discern on how your beliefs may make a difference in your life.

The executives had different opinions on the subject of faith. I received some contrasting feedback on how faith plays a role in their lives and success. Some said it has no role, while others said faith guides all their decisions and is the foundation leaned on to set forth their actions and charter their courses. However, one constant through all of the executives' feedback was the importance of living life by the golden rule. That is,"Do unto others as you would have done unto yourself." Or said another way, "Treat others the way you would like to be treated." This is the most basic tenant of all faith teachings. In short, love one another.

The executives noted that living out the golden rule makes all the difference in your life. For example, one executive noted, "Having faith is important because it's about seeing how we are all connected. With a faith perspective, you see the big picture. With that, it's important to respect many faiths and many beliefs. We all share one thing in common: We are all connected and have the golden rule. Live by the golden rule. At the end of the day, we are all judged by what we do." To conclude on the importance of the golden rule I offer this quote by Molly Friedenfeld, author of the book *Simple Human Truths*,"Golden Rule Living is the great simplifier. It places us in another soul's shoes, taking what can appear to be a complex decision that involves another and streamlining it to a one-step process of deciding, *If I wouldn't like this done to me, then I shall not do it to another.*"

To some executives, faith comes down to simply treating others with respect and having integrity in all you do. Having faith in other people and showing them you believe in them was noted as important too. For others, faith could be summarized by the motto, "You reap what you sow," or the sense of karma. Believing in karma is the notion that if you put good things out into the universe then good things will come back to you. For example, do a good thing for others and good things from others will flow back to you.

For one executive it was his Catholic Christian upbringing that instilled accountability, responsibility, and a calling to a higher purpose and standard. He noted with a smile, "I was raised Catholic so the good old 'Catholic Guilt' has helped ensure I always delivered on what I said

I was going to do. It made me work with integrity and honesty. Having faith also encourages you to do what is right and ethical. Faith, good values, and principles will permeate all you do and it sticks with you."

Another executive provided a clear perspective on faith in stating simply, "You are not alone. The guy upstairs is a pretty big one." He went on to suggest some things with this belief in mind, "Pray and ask. Pray for direction and to be on the right path. Pray to face the right way and ask for help to do the right things." Faith was specifically important to this executive because it helped him settle things down and stay grounded. Faith can help you keep a healthy perspective and it gives you purpose. Faith also pulls you through the hard times and puts life into proper view. Lastly, one executive said seeing faith in others and knowing it's guiding their conduct is like the "Good Housekeeping Seal of Approval." It helps build trust and a comfort level between people, which are key to successful relationships.

Overall, living your life by the golden rule and

respecting the faiths of others was the most common theme shared. Based on the executive feedback, if you are looking to emulate the traits that contributed to their success, it will be good to question how faith plays a role in your life. As noted by most executives, faith helps give a healthy perspective and good lens to view the world and life. This can be helpful to how you perceive your own success and then in turn the decisions you make. This book is all about your success, so asking yourself what measure you are going to use to gauge your success can be helpful. Is your success defined by worldly views or is your success bench marked to a higher faith-based perspective? Knowing can make all the difference.

"The businessman who has faith is not very likely to go wrong. He is going to steer his ship of commerce through the troubled waters of misfortune, perhaps even adversity, with a serenity born of the consciousness that nothing can harm him permanently so long as he sees clearly and acts wisely. There will be many hands eager to retard his progress. Slander will raise its ugly head from many little by-ways along his path. Ill health may come; the loss of

love ones; the crippling of his finances; the striking down of his most cherished hopes; and yet — the man who has Faith — who believes that right is right will triumph."

—Jerome P. Fleishman

 ## Executive Corner

- What is the role of faith in your life?

- Regardless of where you stand on your faith, everyone recommends to live by the golden rule,": "Do unto others as you would have done unto yourself."

- Treat others with respect and have integrity in all you do.

Part Five:
Contributors' Favorite Quotes

Quotes are the most powerful way to impart wisdom in the quickest way possible. They are like skimming the cream off the top of any subject matter to get the most delicious knowledge taste in the shortest communication path. You could say quotes are like the Cliff's Notes of wisdom.

Quotes serve us in two great ways. First, by embracing a wise saying and implementing the knowledge in our lives it can help steer our actions for a better life. And secondly, as the famous French Renaissance writer, Michel de Montaigne, said, "I quote others in order to better express myself." Quotes can be a great way to improve our communication with others to make points more clear. Quotes can also serve as a communication laser to affect good change. Enjoy these quotes. Embrace them where applicable for your life and share them with others if and when appropriate to serving and helping others.

Chapter 11.
Quotes & Meanings

"Only the paranoid survive."

—Andy Grove, President Intel

This quote was provided by Joe Weber, Global Director of Product Line Management at NeoPhotonics Corporation. It speaks to the constant need to keep alert and forever be on guard to your competitive threats. The notion is that everyone is out to eat your lunch in the Valley so you need to be constantly improving, innovating, and delivering the best you can. The Japanese have an interesting saying that I believe is relative to this;it's called "Kaizan." This is an approach and philosophy to execute with continuous innovation. You must always be on the move toward improving and doing things better each day. You may have heard that you are never maintaining equilibrium in business. You are either moving forward or falling behind so you must ensure you make a constant effort to keep progressing forward.

Joe also alluded to another quote that is important to note when trying to succeed and it's relative to this one by Andy Grove. The quote comes from Satchel Paige, and in essence notes: "Never look back, someone might be gaining on you." This speaks about the need to do your job, focus, and keep your eyes on the prize. March forward, execute, and don't look back or you can lose momentum or get distracted to the detriment of your success at hand. This reminds me of the story you may have heard about what famous platoon leaders did upon entering the coastline shores of their enemy. They would burn their boats behind them and say there is only one way to win and retreat is not an option.

Bottom Line: Only the paranoid survive. Keep a healthy dose of paranoia in your diet to keep you pushing hard to stay ahead of your competition. Then focus hard on your execution to keep leading!

"There is no 'I' in TEAM."

—Anonymous

This quote was provided by Charles Whyte, Senior Director at Western Digital. It speaks to the fundamental fact that you really need a team to succeed. There is no "I" in team makes it clear that it's not about you, but the collective body that makes the ultimate success happen. It helps you keep this perspective in mind so you keep your ego in check. We can all live a better life humbly if we remember that saying, "Check your ego at the door." Give credit to others who share in your accomplishments.

One can also learn from this quote to keep the team first, before yourself. Always look for the angle on what you can do to improve the team and work hard to get along and support others. Be a positive force to the team and help everyone succeed. Remember that adage, "The whole is greater than the sum of its parts." A great team made up of the right people, in the right positions, with the right chemistry, is the most powerful force in business.

If you don't think that teams are far superior in producing more creative ideas and outputs, then take an individual look at the facts. Numerous studies show that the output of a team and the decisions made far outperform any individual working on the problem solo.

You may have heard the sarcastic retort, "Oh yeah? Well there ain't no 'We' in team either." While this brings humor to the original quote it's simply that —humor without substance behind it. The fact is, teams are the most important aspect to businesses succeeding. You being a good team member is not only critical to your personal success, but to the ultimate good of the company too.

Bottom line: Recognize the importance of teams, be a great team player, and make your team the best it can be! There is no "I" in team!

"If I were given one hour to save the planet, I would spend 59 minutes defining the problem and one minute resolving it."

—Albert Einstein

This quote was provided by Kevin Conley, SVP and GM of SSD at SanDisk. It reflects the vast importance of thinking things through deeply up front. The point is, the better you can identify the problem, understand the issue at hand, and articulate it, the easier it will be to solve. By knowing the problem very well, the solution can become more obvious. You will be amazed at how what seems like a big problem, once fully understood, only requires a simple solution. This is the smart and successful way to approach a problem versus half-knowing a problem and then trying to come up with an elaborate scheme to fix it.

You may have heard the famous quote by Dorothea Brande relative to this concept: "A problem clearly stated is a problem half solved."Albert Einstein embraced this methodology in his thinking style. It also points to the importance of focusing your energy and time in the right place with the right critical thinking. And lastly, it pushes the point home of doing the smart heavy lifting up front. As Abraham Lincoln said, "Give me six hours to chop down a tree and I will spend the first four sharpening the axe."

Bottom line: Put your finger clearly on the problem, then you can put your hand on the most optimal solution! Put in the hard critical thinking up front, sharpen your tools, and then execute!

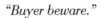

"Buyer beware."

—Anonymous

This short quote was offered by Matt Kaufman, President of CrunchBase. It's been around a long time and dates back to the Latin, caveat *emptor*. It's a very meaningful phrase that helps you keep in mind the importance of being careful of what you hear and to always discern the information you are being fed. You probably heard the connotation this quote as it relates to the phrase, "If it sounds too good to be true, it probably is." This is a helpful point to guiding you away from falling into sales gimmicks and marketing ploys that feed fluff information that in reality can leave you hanging high and dry.

However, in the context offered by Matt, the phase takes on an additional meaning. Matt suggested that whenever you hear someone say, "I'm 80 percent sure about this strategy," or, "I'm 98 percent positive this course of action will succeed," be careful. This phrase is often a red flag. The good business lesson that Matt points out is that in strategy there is no clear certainty. When it comes to the likelihood of success with strategy the answer cannot be put into a percentage. Sales and a strategy is all hogwash until the money really comes in and the steps charted out along the way are actually achieved. It's important to keep a healthy level of skepticism when reviewing strategies. Matt further noted that it's OKto be opportunistic and positive overall, but you must always be rational, realistic, and have sound logic to back up everything when making decisions on a plan of action and charting your strategy.

Bottom line: Be a good, healthy skeptic. Be wise and discerning to evaluate the reality of situations based on facts and logic to improve your likelihood of success!

"No Fear"

—Nike

Harry Dickinson, CEO of Fission Stream Technologies, provided this simple yet powerful quote. It has many great lessons for any aspiring entrepreneur or person looking to make an impact in Silicon Valley. It's a self-evident quote, but can be taken for granted if not embraced and infused into one's approach to life and business. The key to succeed in a technology-driven, ever-changing competitive world is to take risks and try new things. At times you have to take the unbeaten path to make a difference and make your mark. As Robert Frost wrote, "...two roads diverged in the road and I took the road less traveled by, and that has made all the difference..."

When you embrace the "No Fear" motto it can help you step outside your comfort zone and blaze your own trail. This can make you stand out and gain valuable experiences to propel your life forward. You must have courage and be able to release fear. It requires a leap of faith to make that jump. We all have fear. Fear is a good thing because it guides and protects us from danger. However, the key is to handle fear, master it, and do something good with it. As the famous quote from my Toastmasters International speaking club goes, "Everyone has a fear to speak in public. Everyone gets butterflies. The key is to make those butterflies fly in formation." The point is to use fear and channel it for a positive outcome. As Harry noted, "You can't be afraid to fail. You need to try new things and figure out what doesn't work. If you're not failing, you're not taking enough risks."

Bottom line: Consider taking a well-calculated risk. Have no fear. Consider Nike and "Just do it." This is how you can breakthrough and achieve your greatest success.

"Manage the way you would like to be managed. Lead the way you would like to be led."

—Craig McHugh

This quote was offered up by Craig McHugh, CEO of Cambridge SoundWorks, and it hits the heart of the golden rule. Treat others the way you would like to be treated. In addition, you must lead by example. You can't be a "do as I say, not as I do" type of person. To be a successful manager and leader you need to walk the talk. You must be the type of manager you would want to work for and be the type of leader you would want to follow. You can't fake being an excellent leader or manager. Either you are or you are not. You must develop the expertise and competency needed to add real value so others can respect you and welcome your management and leadership. At the same time, you must build the important personal traits that make you respected and enjoyable to be around so people will want to follow you.

Bottom line: Be the kind of person you would want to be around and be led by. Build the right expertise and good personal skills necessary to be a high quality person who people look up to and want to follow. Make it easy for others to follow you by being the real-deal leader!

"We're not getting out of this life alive."

—Dick Sanquini

This lighthearted, yet meaningful, quote was provided by Dick Sanquini, Chairman of PixelWorks. At first this quote can be startling and make you do a double take on the meaning, but in short it teaches us to not take everything in life so seriously. Lighten up. When you stop to recognize the reality that we are all going to pass on one day it's clear we need to relax more and keep work stress in perspective. It's similar to another quote you may have heard: "Don't sweat the small stuff because it's all small stuff."

Dick went on to point out that anything difficult before you at work is just a problem or challenge for you to enjoy solving. Keep it all in perspective. It's just a little challenge and not life or death. Be happy and have fun overcoming hurdles. Don't worry so much or put too much pressure on yourself. Anything you pay attention to will get better.

Bottom Line: Just focus on the task at hand, keep everything in proper perspective, do the best you can, have fun with the challenges, and give it your all. Then let the chips fall where they may. Let go. Stop worrying. Lighten up.

"When you're up to your ass with alligators, don't forget your original objective was to drain the swamp!"

—Ted Preston (Toby Preston's father)

This quote was provided by Toby Preston, Senior Director of Sales at Qualcomm. It came from his father. It's one of those unique, funny, and vivid quotes that makes you think twice about the various meanings it can impart. In short, this quote is about keeping your eye on the end goal.

We will all face distractions or "alligators" along our journey, but to ultimately succeed, we must stay focused on the end game, stay the course, and adjust only when necessary. This has a lot to do with focusing on the right things, but also about being persistent and persevering through adversity.

Think of it as an equation. If your goal is X and you are doing step Y to accomplish X, don't let distraction Z get in your way. Deal with Z quickly as a sub-goal to eliminate the obstacle from goal X, but keep your main goal of finishing X in mind. Don't lose sight of that main objective.

Bottom line: Keep all your endeavors in perspective of your prime goal and take the right actions accordingly to accomplish that objective. Adjust your course if and when needed, but keep your eyes on the prize!

"You can make a lot being bullish, you can make a lot being bearish, but pigs always lose!"

—Sam Nicolino

This fun quote was offered up by Sam Nicolino, President and CEO of Adaptive Sound Technologies. Sam's perspective is to not take on more than you can chew. If it sounds too good to be true, it probably is. In addition, always be careful to not get too greedy. It would be wise to adhere to that saying, "A bird in the hand is worth more than two birds in a bush."

This quote also stems from the finance world. In the

investment community it goes, "Bulls make money, bears make money, but pigs just get slaughtered!" Why? In the investment world a bull market is when everything in the economy is great and stocks are rising. If a person is optimistic and believes that stocks will go up, he or she is said to have a "bullish outlook." You can make money being "bullish" by investing smartly and riding the wave.

A bear market is when the economy is bad and stock prices are falling. If a person is pessimistic, believing that stocks are going to drop, he or she is said to have a "bearish outlook." You can make money being "bearish" when stocks are falling by short selling.

The pigs, on the other hand, are high-risk investors looking for the one big score in a short period of time. Pigs buy on hot tips and invest in companies without doing diligence. They get impatient, greedy, and emotional about their investments, and they are drawn to high-risk securities without putting in the proper time to learn about the investments. Professional traders love the pigs, as it's often from their losses that the bulls and bears reap the profits.

Bottom line: Be wise. Don't bite off more than you can chew. Don't take on more than you can really handle. Do your homework, think things through, and be bullish or bearish if need be, but don't ever be the pig. Don't become a ham sandwich!

"It is what it is."

—Anonymous

Hugh Walker, VP at EMC, offered this quote to denote the importance of being realistic. The meaning is similar to the phrase, "calling a spade a spade." From a business perspective it's important to always see the reality and truth in every situation. Being realistic about what's before you and dealing with it head-on is paramount to your success. Saying, "it is what it is" can be helpful to allowing yourself to detach emotionally from a situation and call out the facts objectively. You can then move forward impartially to address the heart of the matter. Additionally, this quote can imply that something is in the past so let it go and move on. Deal with the reality of your current situation the best you can. Lastly, this quote also teaches the importance of clearly understanding what you can and cannot control. The serenity prayer addresses this beautifully: "God grant me the serenity to accept the things I cannot change,courage to change the things I can, and wisdom to know the difference."

Keeping this quote top of mind amidst the ups and downs of life can help you keep a healthy perspective on everything. I like to say when hardships or struggles come your way, try being like a good Teflon cooking pan. With a new Teflon pan everything slips right off and nothing sticks. When eggs hit you and try to stick, be like that Teflon pan and just let it slip right off. Don't let negative comments, actions, or work stuff wear you down. Don't dwell on things. Just let it roll off and move forward anew.

Bottom line: "It is what it is" so just deal with reality, understand what you can and can't control, address things you can affect, and then move upward and onward!

"Good artists copy; great artists steal."

—Picasso

This quote was offered by Russell Brady, Director of Corporate Communications at Adobe. Picasso seems to get credit for saying it first, but it has been referred to by others over the years, including Steve Jobs, which makes it fitting for Russell to offer the quote since he worked with Jobs at Apple.

Picasso said this quote while reflecting on how when artists steal other people's work, it leads to the creation of new art. Fresh art is due in part because of deliberate imitation of previous developments. Many scholars suggest William Shakespeare routinely stole plot lines and scenes from other writers for his own plays. Copying other ideas and refining upon them is one way of creating new things.

This quote is specifically relevant to succeeding and innovating in Silicon Valley. Successful innovation is not just derived from totally new ideas. Rather, success is often won by creating new and better ways stemming from an existing idea. You don't have to build a completely new mouse trap, just build a superior one. For example, Apple was not first with the MP3 player or cell phone, but their iPod and iPhone became wildly successful after they rode the coattails of previous products in the market and then created a superior product and overall solution. The iPod and iTunes ecosystem is a perfect example of success achieved upon the shoulders of previous product offerings.

Bottom Line: To succeed, it helps to see what is already succeeding. Take the core essence of what is good and understand what is lacking to build up something new, novel, and superior. This approach can often be a more efficient and consistent means of succeeding. If your ideas or product ever get copied, remember the wise words of Charles Colton: "Imitation is the sincerest form of flattery."

"Carried the bag."

—Joseph Castillo

This unique saying came from Joe Castillo, GM at Acer Computers. It refers to people who have been in the trenches, shouldering incredible weight/responsibility for a company. For example, people who have done the hard presentations, met with the important buyers and executives to promote the company, and taken the heat for the successes and failures of the business. When you have "carried the bag," you have been on the front lines of the business marketing and selling the company's products. You know what it takes to get the job done and have endured the flights, hotels, rental cars, and other aspects of hitting the pavement to drive success for the company.

The idea is, in business you really want leaders who have "carried the bag" because they know what it takes to succeed. In management positions, these people can really relate to those on the front lines to help guide and lead effectively. With this real-world experience it allows one to optimally and realistically lead others and make the best decisions for the company too.

Bottom Line: Work hard, prove yourself on the front lines, and earn your stripes. This hard work and real experience will enable you to earn yourself a leadership management role. Then you will be more competent and ready to manage a team to lead a business forward. Success is often built upon the great experiences derived from carrying the bag!

"A good leader inspires others with confidence in him; a great leader inspires them with confidence in themselves."

—Unknown

This quote about leadership is a favorite of Carlos Gonzalez, Senior Director at SanDisk. The quote speaks volumes on what makes a great leader. Leadership is about unleashing the power of teams and individuals so they can accomplish great things for the company.

A leader can provide direction and inspiration, but the team is where the power is, and it will be most effective when its members are motivated and confident in their ability to take on big challenges. One of the best things a leader can do is build a good team, create a good culture, and then mentor the team so they are strong in delivering results even after the leader departs.

Bottom Line: This quote states the truism that being a great leader is about your ability to inspire others around you. Specifically, it's about helping others gain confidence in themselves. If you can help others be confident in their talents and believe in their own ability to deliver, then you have created a healthy foundation from which you can build great teams and a positive culture to best serve the company and everyone involved over the long term.

"Good things happen to good people."

—Anonymous

This quote was offered up by Mark Adams, President of Micron Technologies. It's simple yet very meaningful. It can be understood by looking at two angles coming together. First there's the golden rule angle about treating others the way you would like to be treated. By living out the golden rule you will be a good person and do good things. You are then ready for the second angle. This is the angle of karma, whereas positive things come back when you put out positive things. It's the principle of your inflow matches what you outflow. For example, your good intent and good deeds shared will contribute to your future receipt of goodness in kind.

In short, be good. It's good for you. As Jim Rohn says, "Whatever good things we build end up building us." We all become better people through being a light in this world. Another helpful perspective to this message is to be proactive and do something. Don't just sit there and expect good things to fall in your lap. As Anais Nin said, "Good things happen to those who hustle." Make sure you work hard, be proactive, and get things done. It's in that goodness that helps put in motion the positive results to flow back to you.

Bottom Line: Be a good person, do good things, and give it your all. You will then be setup for good things to come back to you. Life will always be full of ups and downs, but at least you are doing your part to give and attract goodness. Be a light!

"There is no elevator to success. You must always take the stairs."

—Anonymous

I submitted this quote. It's a personal favorite of mine and one I have been using in my email signature since working in the Silicon Valley. Its meaning is pretty self-evident; nothing truly good is ever handed to you. You must always work for it. There is no shortcut to genuine success. No smoke and mirrors can make up for hard work, blood, sweat, toil, and tears. As Earl Nightingale stated, "We will receive not what we idly wish for, but what we justly earn. Our rewards will always be in exact proportion to our service." Athletes know this very well because you can't fake running a mile or lifting weights to help train your body to be in peak condition. You either do or do not, then get the results accordingly!

On the flip side, nothing handed to you without being earned can be fully satisfying. There is a sense of accomplishment and elation that goes alongside of giving your all and leaving everything you got on the playing field. Then when you get the reward you're much more appreciative to really enjoy the prize.

Bottom Line: Don't fake it 'til you make it. That will lead you down a bad path. To achieve true success there is no substitute for good old-fashioned hard work and genuine quality effort. Skip the allure of the elevator and take the stairs. You will make it to the top quicker, better, and stronger!

"A cluttered desk is a cluttered mind."

—Albert Einstein

This quote was shared with me from my father, Michael Washo. Though he is no longer with us, this quote he shared lives on. He would say this often to me and my brothers when we were kids. We had desks in our rooms and our rooms would frequently get messy. When our father told us to clean our rooms, do our homework, and organize our desks we would usually complain. He would reply, "Hey...a cluttered desk is a cluttered mind. Clean it up so you can think straight." The wisdom of this quote is clear. When you are organized and together in your mind and life then the things around you should reflect that. If you are living in a mess, then inside you may be a mess. Having everything straight and in order around you is a reflection of yourself, your mind-set, and your ability to be at your best.

My dad spent his whole career as an engineer working for Eastman Kodak in Rochester, NY. He had that engineering mentality where everything is done for a reason and with sound logic. There is a right way and wrong way of doing things. This perspective is helpful to you being an effective person. Being well-organized is just one part of being most efficient in your life. It helps to think about what is the best way to do something and then do it. As my father would also say, "Measure twice, cut once."

Bottom line: We are often a product of our environment. Our surroundings impact us. If we want to be the most efficient and productive person we can be, especially in our work environment, we should have our desks and things organized. This helps us think and work most efficiently. So keep your things and your environment nice and neat. It's good for you!

Part Six.
The Heart of Success The Recap...

Chapter 12.
Conclusion

If you take the wisdom shared by the Silicon Valley executives, add in the quotes, and embrace their meanings, you will have an accurate blueprint for how to build a great successful life. The final catalyst to making this great kind of success come true for you will ultimately boil down to three points.

First, you must put in the sincere effort to work hard and deliver good results. The cartoon at the beginning of this section humorously depicts how being lucky contributes to success, but ultimately it's a matter of putting in the hard work. This quote makes the relative point, "The harder I work, the luckier I get." In order to be successful you have to roll up your sleeves and put in the effort. There is no shortcut. Nothing great was ever achieved without great effort. Don't be afraid of hard work. As shared previously by Thomas Edison said, "Opportunity is missed by most people because it is dressed in overalls and looks like work." Also, do the work necessary to be the best you can be. Be fully alive, enriched with good quality experiences, endowed with wisdom, and embodied in goodness that enables you to offer real value to others.

Secondly, you need the right fuel and the passion that will help drive you to put in the work necessary to build up this bedrock of success in a way that is healthy, wealthy, wise, and sustainable. How do you get this fuel and passion? Do what you love! Enjoy what you do and the success will follow. Love your work and it becomes easier to do. As the executives all said, you must be passionate. Your light shines brightest when you are doing your calling. How do you know what your calling is? It's when you are doing something you love, tapping into your natural talents, and shining bright while sharing your gifts with others. If you are doing something you love you will notice that time flies. If hours go by like minutes, you are most likely doing something related to your calling.

Lastly, keep your life and success into perspective so you can always make good decisions and react in a positive way to the circumstances that arise. Keep the bigger picture and higher calling perspective in mind. "Don't sweat the small stuff because it's all small stuff." As Dick Sanquini said, "Don't take yourself too seriously. We are not getting out of this world alive." Leave others and the world a better place because of you. Remember, you only have one chance to do it right in this world. You don't get a second chance to make a first impression and you don't get a second chance to live your life over again. This time that you have is the real deal, so live your life with significance.

This poem, "The Dash" by Linda Ellis, helps put all of this into perspective and hits upon the main message this book aims to impart as it relates to the "Heart of Success". You have to have the big picture in mind and think long down the road on how your life is lived and what you will leave behind after you pass. After you have come and gone from this place, how did your life make a difference both professionally and personally? For me it's leaving behind a positive message, sharing my music that I hope moves people in good ways, and leaving behind a life example that had significance. This poem is worth a read and I also recommend sharing it with others. Soak it in and think about how it makes you perceive your precious time here on Earth.

The Dash

by Linda Ellis

I read of a man who stood to speak
at the funeral of a friend.
He referred to the dates on her tombstone
from the beginning…to the end.
He noted that first came the date of her birth
and spoke of the following date with tears,
but he said what mattered most of all
was the dash between those years.
For that dash represents all the time
that she spent alive on earth
and now only those who loved her
know what that little line is worth.
For it matter not, how much we own,
the cars…the house…the cash.
What matters is how we live and love
and how we spend our dash.
So think about this long and hard;
are there things you'd like to change?
For you never know how much time is left
that can still be rearranged.
If we could just slow down enough
to consider what's true and real
and always try to understand

the way other people feel.
And be less quick to anger
and show appreciation more
and love the people in our lives
like we've never loved before.
If we treat each other with respect
and more often wear a smile…
remembering that this special dash
might only last a little while.
So when your eulogy is being read
with your life's actions to rehash,
would you be proud of the things they say
about how you spent your dash?

In conclusion, you have one shot in life. Now is your time. This is your moment. You can grow and improve. They say in life we are either going up or going down. There is no floating in the status quo. Gravity is always at work pulling us down so to move upward and onward we must take action. I will leave you with parting advice from the executives interviewed for this book when asked for final thoughts on succeeding in Silicon Valley. Now it is up to you. Embrace all the advice shared throughout the book and points summarized here. Look to apply them where applicable for the betterment of your life. May you be blessed moving forward with a better life both personally and professionally. May you achieve a great kind of success. Enjoy!

- Enjoy what you do. Do things because you want to. Love it. People will follow and success will grow from there.

- You only go around this place once. Make sure you are doing something you enjoy. Be happy!

- Do the right things. Care about what you do and how it impacts others.

- Stay positive and good things will happen.

- Serve others. Help people. Do your best to make a difference. Share your success!

- Keep a balance between work, life, health,and faith. You need the balance to be a happy and complete person.

- Don't forget who you are and where you come from.

- Stay humble. Stay grounded!

- Be persistent. Keep at it. Keep swinging. Don't give up.

- Be in control of your destiny. Make things happen. Get it done! (GID)

- Resist complacency. Keep learning, doing, and growing.

- If people you trust, and people who trust in you, won't invest in your idea, it's probably not the best idea. Trust your respected circle's feedback.

- Be passionate. Enjoy it, love it, live it, be it, do it!

- Recognize that teams make you successful. You are one of the team. You are only as good as your people.

- Be part of the group and team dynamic. Contribute your best and get along with others. Seek out good teams and good people to work with.

- Be open to learning from everyone. Be a student of life.

- Excel in your profession. Be an expert in something and deliver! Add real value to your company. Look for ways to contribute!

- Take calculated risks.

- Know when to move on...

- Believe in what you do. In order to be successful you have to be in 100 percent. You have to have conviction in what you do and offer all you got.

- Be flexible. Wear many hats and have the ability to change hats based on the people you meet with and communicate to.

- Be resourceful. Acquire the right knowledge, expertise, and skills so you can deliver maximum value.

- Be driven and proactive. Make things happen. Be a self-starter and go-getter!

- Life is a result of a series of choices. Your decisions plot your course. Your choices are very important. When you make decisions in life take the time to discern, understand all, and think about it. If you don't have all the right data, it's better to hold off until you get more information versus rushing towards a bad decision. Think about all deeply.

Part Seven:
About the Contributors

"No one who achieves success does so without the help of others. The wise and confident acknowledge this help with gratitude."

—Alfred North Whitehead

(Common traits these executives embody in keyword form)

(Hardworking, honest, straightforward, humble, confident, smart, fun, nice, strong, quick-witted, experienced, creative, good with people, strong listeners, funny, intelligent, proactive, get it done attitude, excellent communicators, effective, cool, calm, collected, wise, educated, responsible, respectful, generous, team players, disciplined, faithful, passionate, driven, adaptive, visionary, good listeners)

Matt Kaufman

Matt Kaufman is the president of CrunchBase and serves as a partner at a start-up incubator. Matt has been involved with numerous start-ups and is well connected in the Valley with an incredible read on the pulse of all things tech.

I have been fortunate to cross paths professionally with Matt while running the start-up I founded: Amazing Tech Products Inc. Matt was a valuable mentor to me. Additionally, we crossed paths professionally via discussions around his business ventures relating to TV shopping companies like QVC and ShopNBC. Lastly, I know Matt personally since he married my cousin, Karen Mariasi.

Matt is one of those guys that you can tell is brilliant within the first sentence of his communication. You are always left intrigued by his almost uncomfortable pauses when he thinks deeply about questions and then shares forth his always insightful perspective. Matt has a great ability to articulate big, intricate concepts in very clear simple sentences. He can always get to the point succinctly with very few words, yet he imparts deep wisdom. Matt also always imparts this good knowledge in a lighthearted and simple way that makes his points easy to understand. He has a calm, cool, and collected demeanor that exudes confidence. If you ever want great no-nonsense advice and real-world wisdom on start-ups and business success in Silicon Valley, Matt Kaufman is your guy!

Mark Adams

Mark Adams is the president of Micron Technologies. At the time of our interview he was leading his 30,000-plus person company to over $13 billion in revenue while also driving the business to be one of the best growth stocks on NASDAQ. To say he is an accomplished leader and executive is an understatement. He really is the best of the best. I have been fortunate to cross paths with Mark while working together at Creative Labs. Mark was an excellent sales leader who constantly inspired me and played an instrumental role in my career development in both sales and marketing.

Mark is one of those guys that you are impressed with just standing in the same room. He has that special leadership aura and charisma that beams. The great thing is his charisma is backed up with the real deal in smarts, strong communication, and great execution style. Another thing you will find fascinating about Mark is his great outgoing personality that makes him very easy to get along with. At the same time he has the keen ability to be serious, strong, and lay down the hammer when appropriate. He always kept the important business matters front and center to ensure all gets accomplished. He keeps you at the edge of your seat always wanting to perform your very best while also enjoying the ride along the way. When looking for one of the best executives in the Silicon Valley, Mark Adams shines!

Kevin Conley

Kevin Conley is a SVP and GM at SanDisk. I have been fortunate to cross paths with Kevin while working together at SanDisk. I was driving product marketing for the SanDisk MP3 player business while Kevin led engineering. In addition, on a personal level I know Kevin from playing soccer together on various teams where his excellent management skills crossed over to leading soccer clubs. Lastly, Kevin is an excellent musician, guitarist, and singer and I have been fortunate to sync up with him a few times with my piano playing.

Kevin makes the most immediate impression on you because of his great "get it done" leadership style, yet he is always a fun person to be around. Kevin is really fascinating because he has an excellent calm and quiet demeanor about him that keeps everything productive while at the same time he carries an explosive amount of expertise, success, and knowledge, as well as a bright personality to boot up all executions. He has that very unique and special communication style that always makes you lean in and want to listen. It always amazes me how he can be so wonderfully unassuming at times yet be so powerful as a great leader and manager. He has an excellent education and great career track record to back up his success, but is always nice and humble. He really is one to admire, and one of the best guys to have a great chat with about anything in life and business. If you ever want a great chat about life and business over a beer, Kevin is your man.

Harry Dickinson

I had the opportunity to work with Harry when he was VP of Sales at Bigfoot Networks. Harry is a well-rounded person with a wealth of experience from starting companies, leading corporations, getting businesses acquired and sold, and driving success at established companies. All of this enables him to have a vast perspective on business, a strong vision of what's needed to win, and the right moves to position a company for ultimate success. Harry is a professional who proved himself numerous times. When we won business at Bigfoot Networks he was calm, cool, and collected as if everything was part of the plan. One time when I got excited about an opportunity, he told me something that stood out and demonstrated his cool style and advice. Harry said, "Keith, be like Jerry Rice. When you score a touchdown, act like you've been there before."

Harry has a keen ability to explain details of business in colorful ways. At times you feel like a student getting a lecture from a professor. Harry fills you in with stories and anecdotes providing deep insights to every business situation. In addition, Harry has a great perspective on all. I remember when we were in a stressful time at the start-up and were juggling a lot with our professional and personal lives. He said, "Remember your life should always be aligned first with your god, your family, your country, and then the company." I thought this one sentence spoke volumes about him as a great individual, leader, and person to work for. He is truly an outstanding executive and individual.

Craig McHugh

Craig McHugh is the CEO of Cambridge SoundWorks, a company that offers some of the best speaker systems at the most competitive price points. I have been fortunate to cross paths with Craig when he was president of Creative Labs. I worked in sales and marketing for various digital music products under his leadership.

Craig is one of the fastest thinkers you will ever meet. He has the ability to digest what you are saying very quickly and then give back a very straight response that is always on the money. Additionally, if you're looking for someone who has that trait called charisma, Craig is your guy. He has a great presentation and communication style that keeps you on the edge of your seat. He knows how to say the important things, even the hard and difficult aspects of business, in a way that keeps you positive and fired up to do more.

One of the most impressive things I experienced with Craig was his ability to communicate new business opportunities and products with sincere enthusiasm. He really made you feel that every new product was going to be a hit (or, as he says, "Fantastic!"). Under Craig's leadership you got the impression that any new business venture could be the next big thing for the company. He was a strong and firm leader who managed a lot of people and dealt with many changes, but was able to do so in a good style that left a positive impression. He truly is a great leader.

Charles Whyte

Charles Whyte is the Senior Director for one of the best storage companies in the world, Western Digital. I had the opportunity to cross paths with Charles while working together at SanDisk. I was in product marketing for the SanDisk audio/video division while Charles was leading operations. In addition, on a personal level, Charles and I crossed paths with our shared passions for soccer and music. Charles is an accomplished guitarist, singer, and musician.

Charles is a great guy. With one chat you are left impressed with his very kind and charming ways. He is so good at getting along with people that he becomes a friend instantly. He also has that great British accent, which make all his points sound so much more intelligent. In addition, his sense of humor and quick wit make him a joy to be around. You can see his passion for many things, from music and sports to driving business. What stands out the most is his high energy and enthusiasm, which is contagious. He is the positive leadership type that every business needs to help make for a better team and work place. He also is a pro at the motto, "Work hard and play hard." If you are looking for the art of balance in your personal and professional life, then Charles is your guru!

Russell Brady

Russell Brady is the Director of Corporate Communications at one of the best software companies in the world, Adobe. I had the opportunity to get to know Russell on a personal level through being teammates on an indoor soccer team in Silicon Valley. Russell was one of our top goal scorers and his creative and magical play got him nicknamed, "The Wizard." I also had the privilege to work with Russell when leading the start-up company Amazing Tech Products Inc., because Adobe provided some Photoshop software samples for the company to review, award as prizes, and use in its web publishing phase.

What is striking about Russell is his "fun guy to be around" style and his cool Scottish accent. He is the ideal teammate. Behind this great-guy allure is a very smart and quick-witted man with a wealth of experience in succeeding at tech companies. He was an employee at Apple when Steve Jobs came back to the company and worked directly with Steve. He can tell you a great story like no other. Russell, while being a very nice guy, also has leadership strength and a compelling way of being serious when needed,which makes you stand up and listen. He also has a remarkable no-bull style which allows him to always confidently tell it like it is. There are very few PR people in Silicon Valley who have Russell's vast tech experience, great personality, straight-shooting style, and the smarts to back it all up. If you ever want to have a pint and be fascinated by Silicon Valley stories, Russell is your go-to guy!

Toby Preston

Toby Preston is the senior director of sales for the world's leading wireless technology company, Qualcomm. I work with Toby professionally in the Qualcomm Atheros division of the company. While we serve on different teams, since he leads sales and I'm in marketing, Toby always makes you feel part of the same team. This is one example of his great leadership style and excellent charisma. He exemplifies the motto, "Get along with people."

What is most striking about Toby is his down-to-earth mannerism, hard work ethic, and straight up style that always marches toward, "Let's get it done." Perhaps his nice aura stems from his humble Pennsylvania roots, but whatever the reason is, it's refreshing.

Toby is the type of guy that you can enjoy a great laugh with at one moment and then be totally focused on addressing a business problem at another. He is one of those leaders with that keen ability to observe an intricate business scenario and then connect the dots. He is always one of the first to jump in with a creative and feasible solution to a problem. Additionally, Toby communicates very well and looks you straight in the eye. This always leaves a great impression of his trustworthiness. When you think of a good, smart, straight shooter, you think of Toby Preston.

Hugh Walker

Hugh Walker is the Vice President, X-BU Engineering Operations, leading one of the world's most innovative technology and information management companies, EMC. I had the opportunity to work with Hugh at Creative Labs on the internet marketing team.

What you love about Hugh is his philosophical deep thinking style and well organized approach. When he explains things, you know why he always seems to be pondering all so intently. At times he speaks poetically with a quick wit that shows a strong level of understanding and keen ability to articulate very well. Hugh is also very methodical, which helps him always get to the point and clearly address the issue at hand. With Hugh, you always get the sense that nothing will fall through the cracks and that he is on top of it!

You could say Hugh is accountable and responsible to near perfection. Another nice attribute to Hugh's style is his excellent ability to listen. He always allows you to share everything openly. Lastly, he has a good way of supporting you and giving the freedom needed to accomplish tasks with your own style. He knows how to give space and manage effectively. If you want a deep conversation about people, things, and managing, Hugh is your guy.

Joe Weber

Joe Weber is the global director of product line management at NeoPhotonics Corporation. NeoPhotonics is the leading designer and manufacturer of photonic integrated circuit based modules and subsystems for bandwidth-intensive, high-speed communication networks. I had the opportunity to work with Joe at SanDisk in their audio/video division.

Joe is the type of executive who can say the most intelligent things, but makes everything easy to understand. And what stands out is how he can communicate all with a smile. Have you ever met a mentor at work who for some reason has traits that remind you of your father? Joe is that type of guy. In my case, my father was an engineer and lifer at Kodak so he had the glasses, short hair, and ironed-out business shirt appeal. Joe has that same buttoned-up quality. When he talks to you he has that very unique, genuine nature that makes you feel like you're part of the family. You always get a warm impression that you can trust his input and that he is providing you the most solid information in the best interests of all parties involved.

Joe also has that good leadership ability of wearing many hats, rolling up his sleeves, and getting the job done come hell or high water! Lastly, Joe just exudes "smart," so you always feel good about embracing his input and trusting his feedback.

Dick Sanquini

Dick Sanquini is the chairman for PixelWorks. It's hard to find a more experienced, well educated, and accomplished person in Silicon Valley than him. Being able to meet and interview Dick was such a blessing. We share mutual friends who recommended Dick to be a contributor to this book. What a great recommendation because Dick is an all-star.

Dick is one of the few technology executives who played a key role in the birth of the semiconductor industry and the consumer electronics revolution of the 21st century. When you talk with him, his wealth of experience shines bright. He's the type of guy you can sit with for hours relishing his great stories. After talking with Dick for over an hour about succeeding in the Valley, it felt like minutes. Dick has a great level of depth, expertise, and wisdom. What is specifically fascinating about Dick is his seasoned, tenured, and accomplished career, yet great youthfulness despite his golden years. When he shares his experiences he comes across like a young college graduate. He really beams brightly! Dick is also a warm and kind person. Even with all his success and accomplishments he still exudes the aura of a next door neighbor. He displays that nice sense of humility. Overall it's an honor to be around him. After hearing him speak and learning about all his experiences it's clear why he is such a highly respected executive. If you ever get the opportunity to have a meeting with him, cancel any conflicting plans and do it. You're guaranteed enlightenment!

Carlos Gonzalez

Carlos Gonzalez is a senior director at SanDisk helping to lead their Enterprise SSD Firmware endeavors. Being able to interview Carlos was special to me because he is so humble. He suggested kindly that he may not be the right fit to be interviewed for this book. I found this astonishing because Carlos is not only a senior level director at one of the biggest tech companies in the world, but also has an advanced education to boot with his MBA from Santa Clara University. In addition, Carlos is a successful person on the personal side with a long-standing marriage and a family.

Carlos exemplifies one of the common success themes in this book, that is, the importance of humility. Carlos is nice and down-to-earth. He is probably one of the smartest people in the room, but will be the first to tell you he's not. I think his humble nature is inspirational and one of the many reasons he has done so well growing his career. I worked with Carlos at SanDisk in different departments. I recall every encounter with him being pleasant and productive. He always greeted you with a smile. You got the impression he really knew his stuff inside and out.

Carlos is also a guy who takes time to listen and show you support. When I was launching my start-up company, he took time for lunches and offered a listening ear. He is a giving, smart, humble, and kind person. You could say, in short, he's a class act. If you are interested in seeing the full success package, Carlos is your guy!

Sam Nicolino

Sam Nicolino is president and CEO of Adaptive Sound Technologies, where I supported some of his aims to get the Sound+Sleep products listed with resellers like Newegg.com, NCIX, and HSN TV.

Sam has a wealth of Silicon Valley experience from working with many of the Valley's most famous companies like National Semiconductor, Intel, Atari, Sun, and NVIDIA. Sam is a very bright engineer at heart and a great entrepreneur. He is one of the smartest guys you will meet yet is so nice and soft spoken. He is a kind and humble guy. Sam is also a father and grandfather so he also has that nice family guy appeal. However, don't let this calm demeanor fool you because he's tough as nails when it comes to making a business successful and scrapping it out to do the right things in the right way for products. Sam is the kind of guy who doesn't like to cut corners and always thinks things through.

Sam runs his business very smart with few resources. This goes to show the talent he has in being able to do so much with so little. He's also an accomplished keyboardist and has a nice creative music side to him too. All of this talent pays off dividends in his ability to create innovative products. He has clever ideas and the know-how to create and market unique products. If you're looking for a great guy to give you a well-rounded perspective on technology, innovation, and Silicon Valley, then Sam's your man.

Joe Castillo

Joe Castillo is the GM for Acer Computers of Latin America. I crossed paths with Joe in our work together on the sales team at Creative Labs. He was one of the star sales managers handling some of the toughest retailers, and doing it all with great style and salesmanship.

Joe is a great example of what this book is all about. He exemplifies the good kind of well-rounded success. Joe is a great role model for succeeding in the Valley the wholesome way. He is a great husband, father, athlete, and executive while doing all of his various roles with class. If you look at how Joe achieved his success, it came from hard work, quality effort, and a strong focus to hone his craft and deliver results. He truly worked his way up the ranks and has lived out the quote, "There is no elevator to success; one must always take the stairs." In addition, Joe always has a great smile and the ability to make you laugh. Joe exudes unique charisma which makes you feel like a best friend within minutes of being in his presence.

Joe is leading one of the world's biggest computer companies as an executive yet still finds time to run the Iron Man race, keep in good health overall, and be there for his kids' games. Joe really is a tried and true successful Silicon Valley executive that has earned his keep the good old-fashioned way. If you want to meet a one of a kind hardworking executive, Joe is your man!

Contributors

- Matt Kaufman, President of CrunchBase
- Mark Adams, President of Micron Technologies
- Kevin Conley, SVP and GM of SanDisk
- Harry Dickinson, CEO of Fission Stream Technologies
- Craig McHugh, CEO of Cambridge Soundworks
- Charles Whyte, Senior Director at Western Digital
- Russell Brady, Director of Corporate Communications at Adobe
- Sam Nicolino, President and CEO of Adaptive Sound Technologies
- Joe Castillo, GM of Acer Computers for Latin America
- Toby Preston, Senior Director of Sales at Qualcomm
- Carlos Gonzalez, Senior Director at SanDisk
- Dick Sanquini, Chairman of PixelWorks
- Hugh Walker, Vice President of Engineering Operations at EMC
- Joe Weber, Senior Director of Product Line Management at NeoPhotonics

About the Author

Biography

Keith D. Washo lives in Silicon Valley, where he has worked for over a decade leading technology companies and start-ups. He has been honored by Toastmasters International as an award-winning contest speaker. He also shares in a U.S. patent for digital audio players and is the founder of a consumer electronics business. In addition, Washo is a keyboardist, composer, and publisher of his own music.

He holds an Executive MBA from Saint Mary's College of California, a master's in Music Business and Entertainment Industries from the University of Miami, and a BA in Broadcasting and Music from the State University of New York at Oswego. You can learn more at KeithWasho.com.